PLAY BETTER GOLF:
The Swing From A–Z

Put your game on tournament level.

Strip away the mistakes that lead to slicing and hooking—and a bad game score.

Golf's great, Jack Nicklaus, shows you how to make every shot count by generously offering a comprehensive look at how to execute and achieve a "professional swing."

Here are his ten basics of good technique:

- Swing the same with every club
- Strive for a full arc
- Never try for "topspin"
- Focus strongly on the ball
- Develop a preferred shot "shape"
- Beware of overexperimenting
- Don't be too "position" conscious
- Always fully "wind your spring"
- Use all your resources
- Never forget to *hit* the ball

PLAY BETTER GOLF

THE SWING FROM A–Z

Jack Nicklaus

With Ken Bowden
Illustrated by Jim McQueen

P

PUBLISHED BY POCKET BOOKS NEW YORK

All drawings contained in this work have been previously published by King Features, Inc.

Another *Original* publication of POCKET BOOKS

 POCKET BOOKS, a Simon & Schuster division of
GULF & WESTERN CORPORATION
1230 Avenue of the Americas, New York, N.Y. 10020

ISBN: 0-671-43881-6

First Pocket Books printing July, 1980

10 9 8 7 6 5 4 3 2

POCKET and colophon are trademarks of Simon & Schuster.

Printed in the U.S.A.

Contents

Introduction

Will this book *really* help you play better golf?

Well, to improve at this marvelous but maddening game you must first know what you are doing wrong and then how to make it right. Unless you've got enough time and energy to work things out purely by trial and error, that requires information. The best way to get that information is from a skilled teacher in one-on-one lessons—as I was fortunate to be able to do as a youngster. If that's impractical or unappealing, the next best way is via the printed page—especially when each piece of information is self-contained, to the point and well illustrated, as I hope we've achieved here.

Within these pages I've tried to present all I know about the tee-to-green golf swing as clearly, crisply and logically as possible. That's the most exciting part of golf, and the most demanding. Improving at it even a little bit will give you great inner satisfaction, as well as lower scores. (That's why I'm still always trying to improve, even after thirty years in the game.) In future volumes, we plan to deal in similar style and scope with the art of scoring, which includes the short game, and then with faults, cures and trouble shots.

One word of warning. If you choose to read the book first time around from cover to cover, you'll quickly realize that it contains a large amount of information. Don't try to put everything into effect at once, or even to absorb it all at one reading. Be selective in relation to your own present golfing capabilities and problems, and try always to work on one thing at a time, preferably in a properly ordered sequence. Remember that improving a golf swing or mastering a particular type of shot always takes time and patience, as well as mental know-how and physical effort.

Hopefully, you'll also find the book easy to use for quick refreshers and reminders on specific points, as well as for self-correction.

Finally, a word of appreciation. All the articles herein were originally created for distribution to newspapers worldwide by King Features Syndicate of New York, and I would like to thank my friends at King for their fine efforts in that direction.

Jack Nicklaus

PART ONE

Some Fundamentals

1

Thinking Your Way
to a Better Game

Learn and Stick to Fundamentals

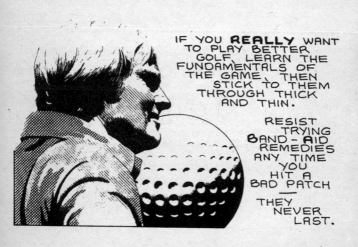

IF YOU **REALLY** WANT TO PLAY BETTER GOLF, LEARN THE FUNDAMENTALS OF THE GAME, THEN STICK TO THEM THROUGH THICK AND THIN.

RESIST TRYING BAND-AID REMEDIES ANY TIME YOU HIT A BAD PATCH — THEY NEVER LAST.

START WITH GRIP AND SET-UP, THEN WORK THROUGH THE REST OF THE BASICS — IN YOUR GENERAL GOLF THINKING, YOUR PLAY, AND ESPECIALLY DURING YOUR **PRACTICE**.

IF YOU DON'T KNOW WHAT THE FUNDAMENTALS ARE, GO SEE A GOOD TEACHING PRO.

Review Your Game Honestly

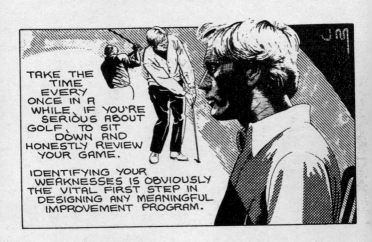

TAKE THE TIME EVERY ONCE IN A WHILE, IF YOU'RE SERIOUS ABOUT GOLF, TO SIT DOWN AND HONESTLY REVIEW YOUR GAME.

IDENTIFYING YOUR WEAKNESSES IS OBVIOUSLY THE VITAL FIRST STEP IN DESIGNING ANY MEANINGFUL IMPROVEMENT PROGRAM.

I DO THIS AT LEAST ONCE A YEAR, BREAKING MY GAME DOWN INTO DRIVING, APPROACHING, RECOVERY PLAY, PUTTING, COURSE-MANAGEMENT AND SELF-MANAGEMENT. HAVING DETERMINED WHERE MY PROBLEMS LIE, I THEN DESIGN AN ACTION PLAN TO TRY TO SOLVE THEM — OFTEN BEGINNING WITH A LESSON FROM MY LIFE-LONG TEACHER, **JACK GROUT**.

A SIMILAR APPROACH MIGHT BRING YOU A LOT MORE SATISFACTION FROM GOLF.

Keep it Simple

Develop Key Swing Thoughts

STRAIGHT LEFT ARM
TURN SHOULDERS 90°
EYES ON BALL
START DOWN WITH
LOWER BODY
RIGHT ELBOW IN
STAY BEHIND BALL
FIRM L- GRIP

IT'S VIRTUALLY IMPOSSIBLE TO THINK OF MORE THAN ONE OR TWO THINGS DURING THE LESS-THAN-TWO-SECONDS IT GENERALLY TAKES TO COMPLETE A GOLF SWING.

SO DON'T CONFUSE YOURSELF BY TRYING TO!

THE TWO THINGS I'VE MOSTLY THOUGHT ABOUT DURING THE EXECUTION OF THE SWING ARE:
1) TAKING THE CLUB STRAIGHT BACK FROM THE BALL AS DELIBERATELY AS POSSIBLE CONSISTENT WITH SWING-ING IT AWAY; AND
2) KEEPING MY HEAD STEADY. WHENEVER I'VE BEEN ACHIEVING ONE OF THESE WITHOUT HAVING TO THINK ABOUT IT, I'VE GENER-ALLY REPLACED IT WITH THE THOUGHT: "COMPLETE THE BACKSWING."

Don't Be Too Proud to Take Lessons

EVERY YEAR I'VE COMPETED AT GOLF, AS AMATEUR AND PROFESSIONAL, I'VE PREFACED THE CAMPAIGN WITH A LESSON FROM MY LIFELONG TEACHER, JACK GROUT.

"JACK," I SAY TO HIM, "I'D LIKE TO TAKE UP GOLF. SHOW ME HOW TO HOLD THE CLUB, HOW TO ADDRESS THE BALL, AND HOW TO SWING."

IN OTHER WORDS, WHAT I'M AFTER IS A COMPLETE REFRESHER COURSE IN THE BASIC FUNDAMENTALS TO ENSURE I'M PROPERLY ON TRACK IN MY UPCOMING PRACTICE SESSIONS. I HAVE TO BELIEVE THE SAME EXERCISE WOULD DO YOU GOOD, TOO.

Be Prepared to Practice

HOW WELL YOU PLAY GOLF ISN'T ENTIRELY A MATTER OF HOW MUCH YOU PRACTICE, BUT THE TWO ARE CLOSELY RELATED.

ONE THING IS FOR SURE: THERE'S NEVER BEEN A GREAT PLAYER WHO DID NOT HIT HUNDREDS OF THOUSANDS OF PRACTICE SHOTS, AT LEAST WHILE HE OR SHE WAS LEARNING THE GAME.

NO TIME OR OPPORTUNITY TO PRACTICE? WELL, WHERE THERE'S A WILL THERE'S A WAY. AS A YOUNGSTER, I'D EVEN PRACTICE IN THE SNOW, CLEARING A SPOT OR HITTING OFF COMPACTED SNOW IF I COULDN'T GET TO GROUND LEVEL. NOT MANY AMATEURS WOULD GO THAT FAR, I ADMIT, BUT THERE'S NOTHING TO STOP YOU AT LEAST SWINGING A CLUB FOR FIVE OR SO MINUTES A DAY WHEN YOU CAN'T GET OUT TO THE COURSE.

Never Hit a "Quit" Shot

PEOPLE OFTEN COMMENT ON MY ABILITY TO CONCENTRATE AND COMPETE HARD EVEN WHEN NOT PLAYING MY BEST.

ONE FACTOR BEHIND THESE ASSETS IS A LIFELONG HABIT OF NEVER HITTING SHOTS CARELESSLY, HALF-HEARTEDLY, OR BAD-TEMPEREDLY.

PERHAPS THE SAME HABIT WOULD HELP YOUR GAME — AND YOUR MENTAL APPROACH. RESOLVE TO GIVE EVERY SINGLE STROKE YOU PLAY YOUR **ABSOLUTE** BEST TRY, IN PRACTICE AS WELL AS IN PLAY.

IN OTHER WORDS, NEVER HIT A "QUIT" SHOT.

2

Ten Basics of Good Technique

Swing the Same with Every Club

THE FULL GOLF SWING REMAINS BASICALLY THE SAME WITH EVERY CLUB IN THE BAG.

YOU'LL AUTOMATICALLY STAND CLOSER TO THE BALL THE SHORTER THE CLUB YOU'RE PLAYING, AND THUS SWING PROGRESSIVELY MORE UPRIGHT.

BUT THERE SHOULD BE NO CONSCIOUS CHANGE IN YOUR OVERALL SWING PATTERN ON ALL NORMAL SHOTS.

Strive for a Full Arc

ONE REASON FULL SWINGERS GENERALLY LAST LONGER THAN SHORT SWINGERS IS THAT THEY CAN STILL MAKE A GOOD, BIG ARC EVEN AS AGE INEVITABLY REDUCES MUSCULAR AGILITY.

ANOTHER REASON IS THAT THE LONGER THE SWING — SO LONG AS IT IS CONTROLLED — THE MORE ROOM YOU HAVE TO ACHIEVE PROPER TIMING AND RHYTHM.

THAT'S WHY I ENCOURAGE MY BOYS TO SWING AS FULLY AS POSSIBLE AS SOON AS POSSIBLE. I ALSO ENCOURAGE THEM TO HIT THE BALL HARD NOW, AND WORRY ABOUT CONTROL LATER.

Never Try for "Topspin"

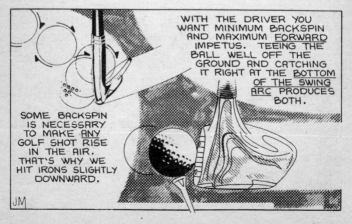

Focus Strongly on the Ball

Develop a Preferred Shot "Shape"

REMEMBER THAT THE REAL SECRET OF GOOD GOLF IS **REPETITION**, AND THAT THE TOUGHEST SHOT TO REPEAT CONSISTENTLY IS A DEAD STRAIGHT ONE.

THAT'S WHY THE PROS EITHER **DRAW** OR **FADE** THE BALL ON MOST SHOTS — OR, IN THE CASE OF THE BETTER ONES HIT IT EITHER WAY AT WILL.

YOU'LL SCORE MORE EFFECTIVELY, TOO, IF YOU CAN LEARN TO CONSISTENTLY FLIGHT THE BALL EITHER FROM LEFT TO RIGHT OR RIGHT TO LEFT.

Beware of Overexperimenting

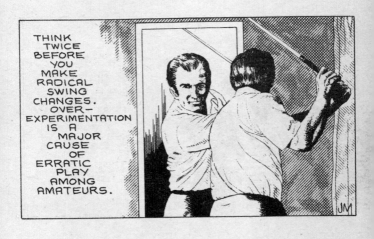

THINK TWICE BEFORE YOU MAKE RADICAL SWING CHANGES. OVER-EXPERIMENTATION IS A MAJOR CAUSE OF ERRATIC PLAY AMONG AMATEURS.

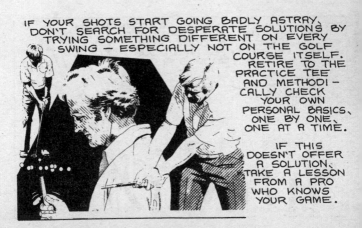

IF YOUR SHOTS START GOING BADLY ASTRAY, DON'T SEARCH FOR DESPERATE SOLUTIONS BY TRYING SOMETHING DIFFERENT ON EVERY SWING — ESPECIALLY NOT ON THE GOLF COURSE ITSELF. RETIRE TO THE PRACTICE TEE AND METHODI-CALLY CHECK YOUR OWN PERSONAL BASICS, ONE BY ONE, ONE AT A TIME.

IF THIS DOESN'T OFFER A SOLUTION, TAKE A LESSON FROM A PRO WHO KNOWS YOUR GAME.

Don't Be Too "Position" Conscious

IN SEEKING IMPROVEMENT BY ANALYZING THE GOLF SWING, AND PARTICULARLY YOUR OWN FORM, BEWARE OF BECOMING TOO "POSITION" CONSCIOUS.

JM

REMEMBER THAT YOU SWING **THROUGH**, NOT TO, THE VARIOUS POSITIONS THAT REPRESENT GOOD FORM, AND THAT TO BE EFFECTIVE YOUR ACTIONS MUST BE A CONTINUOUS AND RHYTHMICAL FLOW OF MOVEMENT. ABOVE ALL, THINK AND FEEL **SWING** ESPECIALLY IN THE CLUBHEAD.

Always Fully "Wind Your Spring"

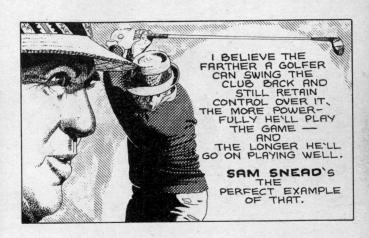

I BELIEVE THE FARTHER A GOLFER CAN SWING THE CLUB BACK AND STILL RETAIN CONTROL OVER IT, THE MORE POWER-FULLY HE'LL PLAY THE GAME — AND THE LONGER HE'LL GO ON PLAYING WELL.

SAM SNEAD'S THE PERFECT EXAMPLE OF THAT.

HOWEVER, NOT EVERYONE HAS THE PHYSIQUE TO SWING BACK AS FULLY AS **SAM**. IF YOU DON'T, FORGET THE ACTUAL LENGTH OF YOUR BACKSWING ARC AND WORK INSTEAD ON **MAXIMUM COILING** OF YOUR UPPER HALF AGAINST THE RESISTANCE OF YOUR LOWER HALF.

EVEN IF THE CLUB ONLY GETS HALF AS FAR BACK AS **SAM**'S, YOU'LL STILL GIVE THE BALL A FINE RIDE IF YOU "WIND THE SPRING" AS HARD AS YOU CAN.

THERE'S A LOT OF TALK THESE DAYS IN GOLFING CIRCLES ABOUT "LEFT-SIDEDNESS" AND "RIGHT-SIDEDNESS" IN THE SWING.

TO ME, THE GAME DEMANDS FULL USE OF **BOTH** SIDES OF THE BODY.

JM

I DON'T BELIEVE A GOLFER CAN USE HIS RIGHT SIDE TOO MUCH SO LONG AS HIS LEFT SIDE **LEADS AND CONTROLS** THE SWING. FOR EXAMPLE, ONCE MY LEFT SIDE HAS INITIATED THE DOWNSWING, WHEN DRIVING I HIT JUST ABOUT AS HARD AS I CAN WITH MY RIGHT SIDE GOING THROUGH THE BALL.

PLAYING WITH ONLY HALF THE BODY, I FEEL, WOULD PRODUCE ONLY HALF THE DISTANCE I NEED ON TEE SHOTS.

Never Forget to <u>Hit</u> The Ball

DON'T GET SO BOUND UP IN SWING THEORY AND 'POSITIONS' THAT YOU FORGET TO **HIT** THE BALL WITH THE <u>CLUBHEAD.</u>

YOU MUST <u>RELEASE</u> THE CLUBHEAD TO HIT THE BALL FAR AND TRUE. WAY TO DO THAT IS START DOWN WITH YOUR LEGS OFF A GOOD, TORQUE-PACKED BACKSWING. THEN **LET GO** FULLY AND FREELY WITH YOUR <u>ARMS</u>, <u>WRISTS</u> AND <u>HANDS.</u>

3

Golf's "Geometry"

Don't Try to Play a Dead Straight Game

YOU'LL RARELY SEE A PRO TRY TO HIT THE BALL DEAD STRAIGHT. REASON IS THAT THE ABSOLUTELY STRAIGHT SHOT IS SO DIFFICULT AS TO BE ALMOST A FLUKE.

HERE'S WHAT YOU MUST DO AT IMPACT TO ACHIEVE THAT FLUKE:
1. YOUR CLUBHEAD MUST MOVE <u>DIRECTLY</u> ALONG YOUR TARGET LINE.
2. YOUR CLUBFACE MUST BE <u>PERFECTLY</u> SQUARE TO YOUR TARGET.
3. YOU MUST HIT THE BALL <u>ABSOLUTELY</u> ON THE CENTER OF THE CLUBFACE.

1.   2.   3.

...AND ALL THAT WITH THE CLUBHEAD TRAVELING AT AROUND 100 M.P.H.!

BECAUSE OF THE IMPOSSIBILITY OF ALWAYS REPEATING THOSE IDEALS, MOST TOUR PROS FAVOR EITHER A DELIBERATE **FADE** OR **DRAW** — THE BEST OF THEM BEING CAPABLE OF EITHER 'SHAPE' AT ANY TIME. THAT SHOULD BE YOUR APPROACH, TOO.

JM

Know What Causes Slices, Hooks...

GOOD GOLF STARTS WITH KNOWING WHAT CAUSES YOUR SHOTS TO CURVE.

SLICING COMES FROM IMPACTING THE BALL WITH YOUR CLUBFACE LOOKING <u>RIGHT</u> OF THE DIRECTION IN WHICH YOUR CLUBHEAD IS TRAVELING.

A **FADE** – MY BASIC SHOT – COMES FROM THE SAME INTERACTION, ONLY THE ANGLE BETWEEN CLUBFACE AND SWING PATH IS **SMALLER**.

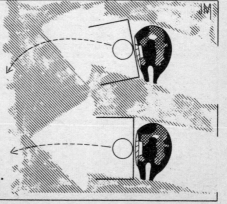

HOOKING COMES FROM IMPACTING THE BALL WITH THE CLUBFACE LOOKING <u>LEFT</u> OF THE DIRECTION IN WHICH YOUR CLUBHEAD IS TRAVELING.

A **DRAW** – THE IDEAL SHOT FOR THE AMATEUR – COMES FROM THE SAME INTERACTION, BUT AGAIN THE CLUBFACE SWING PATH ANGLE IS <u>SMALLER</u>.

...and Pulls and Pushes

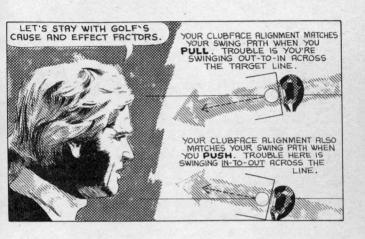

LET'S STAY WITH GOLF'S CAUSE AND EFFECT FACTORS.

YOUR CLUBFACE ALIGNMENT MATCHES YOUR SWING PATH WHEN YOU **PULL**. TROUBLE IS YOU'RE SWINGING OUT-TO-IN ACROSS THE TARGET LINE.

YOUR CLUBFACE ALIGNMENT ALSO MATCHES YOUR SWING PATH WHEN YOU **PUSH**. TROUBLE HERE IS SWINGING <u>IN-TO-OUT</u> ACROSS THE LINE.

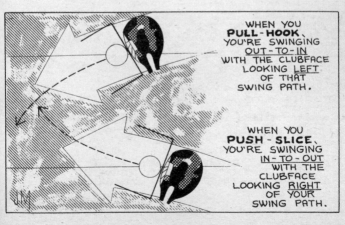

WHEN YOU **PULL-HOOK**, YOU'RE SWINGING <u>OUT-TO-IN</u> WITH THE CLUBFACE LOOKING <u>LEFT</u> OF THAT SWING PATH.

WHEN YOU **PUSH-SLICE**, YOU'RE SWINGING <u>IN-TO-OUT</u> WITH THE CLUBFACE LOOKING <u>RIGHT</u> OF YOUR SWING PATH.

25

Understand These Spin Effects

IN BUILDING YOURSELF A GOLF GAME, KEEP THE FOLLOWING IN MIND.

1) A FADE GIVES MORE CONTROL THAN A DRAW BECAUSE THE BALL FLIES HIGHER, LANDS MORE SOFTLY, AND BREAKS LESS SHARPLY ON IMPACT. HOWEVER, A DRAW GIVES YOU MORE DISTANCE BECAUSE THE BALL FLIES LOWER, LANDS FASTER, AND RUNS FARTHER.

2) IF A FADE TURNS INTO A SLICE, IT WILL SEVERELY REDUCE YOUR DISTANCE. HOWEVER, IF A DRAW TURNS INTO A HOOK, IT WILL OFTEN RUN INTO TROUBLE MORE READILY.

3) GOLF IS EASIEST WHEN YOU PLAY **WITH**, RATHER THAN AGAINST, YOUR NATURAL SHOT-FLIGHTING TENDENCIES.

Fit Your Plane to Your Build

DON'T LET ALL THE TALK AND LITERATURE ABOUT "FLAT" AND "UPRIGHT" SWING PLANES THROW YOU OUT OF YOUR OWN NATURAL SHAPE OF SWING. ACTUALLY, THE DIFFERENCE BETWEEN SO-CALLED FLAT AND UPRIGHT PLANES AMONG GOOD PLAYERS IS GENERALLY ONLY A FEW DEGREES.

IF YOU'RE TALL, YOU'LL NATURALLY STAND FAIRLY CLOSE TO THE BALL AND THUS NATURALLY SWING ON A FAIRLY UPRIGHT PLANE. IF YOU'RE SHORTER, STANDING FARTHER FROM THE BALL WILL NATURALLY CREATE A SOMEWHAT FLATTER PLANE. GO WITH WHAT'S NATURAL, AND DON'T EXAGGERATE.

Have These Angles Checked Out

SHOULD YOU TRY TO SWING ON AN UPRIGHT OR A FLAT PLANE ?

THE SHORT ANSWER IS: DO WHAT COMES MOST NATURALLY, BUT DON'T EXAGGERATE ONE WAY OR THE OTHER.

BEYOND THAT, IT DEPENDS WHAT KIND OF GOLF SHOTS YOU PRIMARILY WANT TO HIT. GENERALLY, THE MORE UP-RIGHT YOUR SWING, THE HIGHER YOU WILL HIT THE BALL AND THE MORE EASILY YOU WILL BE ABLE TO FADE IT. CONVERSELY, THE FLATTER YOU SWING, THE LOWER YOU'LL HIT THE BALL AND THE MORE EASILY YOU WILL BE ABLE TO DRAW IT.

Know the Proper Clubhead Path

MANY GOLFERS GET BACKACHE AND BAD SCORES THROUGH A FUNDAMENTAL MISCONCEPTION OF THE PATH THE CLUBHEAD SHOULD FOLLOW THROUGH IMPACT.

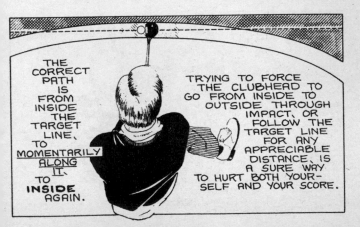

THE CORRECT PATH IS FROM INSIDE THE TARGET LINE, TO MOMENTARILY ALONG IT, TO INSIDE AGAIN.

TRYING TO FORCE THE CLUBHEAD TO GO FROM INSIDE TO OUTSIDE THROUGH IMPACT, OR FOLLOW THE TARGET LINE FOR ANY APPRECIABLE DISTANCE, IS A SURE WAY TO HURT BOTH YOUR- SELF AND YOUR SCORE.

Swing Shaft to Parallel at Top

WHEN THE CLUB POINTS **LEFT** OF THE TARGET LINE AT THE TOP OF THE BACKSWING, IT WILL GENERALLY SWING ACROSS THAT LINE FROM <u>OUT TO IN</u> AT IMPACT.

CONVERSELY, WHEN THE CLUB POINTS <u>RIGHT</u> OF THE TARGET LINE AT THE TOP, IT WILL USUALLY BE MOVING FROM **IN TO OUT** AT IMPACT.

THAT'S WHY I ALWAYS STRIVE NOT TO "CROSS THE LINE" AT THE TOP. WHEN THE CLUB SHAFT <u>PARALLELS</u> THE TARGET LINE THERE, ITS NATURALLY POSITIONED TO SWING <u>ON LINE</u> THROUGH IMPACT.

JM

Don't Manipulate the Clubface

IN A PROPER GOLF SWING, THE CLUBFACE <u>APPEARS</u> TO OPEN AS THE CLUB MOVES AWAY FROM THE BALL, AND <u>APPEARS</u> TO CLOSE AS IT TRACKS THE BALL INTO THE FOLLOW—THROUGH.

ACTUALLY, IT DOES NEITHER UNLESS YOU MANIPULATE IT IN SOME WAY WITH YOUR HANDS AND ARMS.

TO PROVE THE POINT, SWING BACK TO WAIST HEIGHT, THEN TURN SO THAT YOUR BODY FACES DIRECTLY DOWN THE CLUBSHAFT. DO THE SAME AFTER SWINGING TO WAIST HEIGHT IN THE FOLLOW—THROUGH.

IN BOTH CASES, YOU'LL FIND THE CLUBFACE IS IN THE SAME **SQUARE** RELATIONSHIP TO YOUR HANDS AND BODY AS IT WAS AT ADDRESS.

4

Your
Equipment

Let a Pro Help You Pick Clubs

BUYING NEW CLUBS?

UNLESS YOU'RE A GOOD ENOUGH GOLFER TO KNOW FROM EXPERIENCE EXACTLY WHAT YOU WANT, GET THE HELP OF A GOOD TEACHING PRO WHO KNOWS YOUR GAME IN DETERMINING THEIR PLAYABILITY CHARACTERISTICS.

PROPERLY MATCHING YOUR TOOLS TO YOUR TRAITS AND TALENTS — ESPECIALLY IN THE AREAS OF WEIGHT AND SHAFT FLEX — COULD DEFINITELY SAVE YOU A SHOT OR TWO. THAT'S WHY, IF YOU HAVE A FAVORITE CLUB, IT'S A GOOD IDEA TO KNOW ITS SPECIFICATIONS AND USE THOSE AS A GUIDE WHENEVER YOU'RE RE-EQUIPPING YOURSELF.

MANY GOLFERS TALK OF SWINGWEIGHT WITHOUT REALLY UNDERSTANDING WHAT IT MEANS.

ESSENTIALLY, SWINGWEIGHT IS A CONCEPT RELATING THE WEIGHT OF THE GRIP END OF A GOLF CLUB TO ITS HEAD WEIGHT.

JM

BASICALLY, THE HIGHER THE SWINGWEIGHT DESIGNATION THE HEAVIER THE CLUBHEAD WILL FEEL IN RELATION TO THE GRIP END AS YOU SWING. USE THIS CONCEPT AS A GUIDE IN SELECTING CLUBS, BUT DON'T STOP THERE. DEADWEIGHT AND SHAFT FLEXIBILITY ARE ALSO IMPORTANT FACTORS, AND YOU SHOULD OBTAIN PROFESSIONAL HELP IN MATCHING ALL THREE TO YOUR OWN PHYSIQUE AND SWING STYLE.

Match Your Set to Your Ability

THE RULES ALLOW YOU 14 CLUBS. SELECT THEM TO MATCH YOUR PERSONAL ABILITIES, NOT SOME THEORETICAL IDEAL. FOR EXAMPLE, I CARRY A DRIVER, 3-WOOD, IRONS 1 THROUGH 9, PITCHING WEDGE, MODERATELY-FLANGED SAND-WEDGE, AND PUTTER. THAT'S A MIX PERHAPS SUITABLE FOR ANYONE WHO SHOOTS 75 OR BETTER.

IF YOU SCORE MORE THAN A FEW SHOTS HIGHER THAN THAT, HOWEVER, YOU NEED AN "EASIER" SET — SUCH AS, FOR EXAMPLE, DRIVER, 3-, 4-, AND 5- (OR 6-) WOODS, IRONS 3 THROUGH 9, PITCHING WEDGE, DEEP-FLANGED SAND-WEDGE, AND PUTTER.

DON'T LET EGO PREVENT YOU FROM CARRYING CLUBS THAT YOU CAN ACTUALLY PLAY, RATHER THAN ONES THAT SIMPLY LOOK GOOD IN THE BAG.

Experiment to Find Ideal "Specs"

SELECT YOUR CLUBS TO MATCH YOUR PHYSIQUE. BASICALLY, THE HEAVIER A CLUB, THE STRONGER YOU HAVE TO BE TO CONTROL IT AND GENERATE MAXIMUM 'HEAD SPEED.

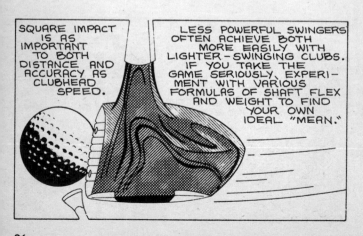

SQUARE IMPACT IS AS IMPORTANT TO BOTH DISTANCE AND ACCURACY AS CLUBHEAD SPEED.

LESS POWERFUL SWINGERS OFTEN ACHIEVE BOTH MORE EASILY WITH LIGHTER-SWINGING CLUBS. IF YOU TAKE THE GAME SERIOUSLY, EXPERIMENT WITH VARIOUS FORMULAS OF SHAFT FLEX AND WEIGHT TO FIND YOUR OWN IDEAL "MEAN."

Take Your Height into Account

DOES A TALL GOLFER NEED LONGER-THAN-STANDARD CLUBS?

IT MIGHT BE WORTH EXPERIMENTING, BUT THE DANGER IS THAT LONGER CLUBS CAN CAUSE A TALL PLAYER TO LOSE CONTROL BY LENGTHENING HIS ALREADY LARGE SWING ARC. PROFESSIONAL COUNSEL IS ADVISABLE.

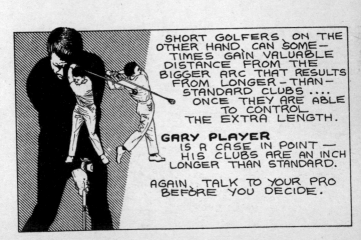

SHORT GOLFERS ON THE OTHER HAND, CAN SOME-TIMES GAIN VALUABLE DISTANCE FROM THE BIGGER ARC THAT RESULTS FROM LONGER-THAN-STANDARD CLUBS .... ONCE THEY ARE ABLE TO CONTROL THE EXTRA LENGTH.

GARY PLAYER IS A CASE IN POINT — HIS CLUBS ARE AN INCH LONGER THAN STANDARD.

AGAIN, TALK TO YOUR PRO BEFORE YOU DECIDE.

Consider Lighter Clubs

ALTHOUGH I'M NOT REALLY FAMILIAR WITH THE SPECIAL PROBLEMS OF SENIOR MEN AND LADY GOLFERS, I'VE OFTEN FELT BOTH MIGHT ENJOY THE GAME MORE BY USING LIGHTER-THAN-NORMAL CLUBS.

VELOCITY HAVING TWICE THE VALUE OF MASS IN TERMS OF DISTANCE, IT SEEMS LOGICAL THAT BOTH GROUPS COULD HIT THE BALL FARTHER WITH CLUBS THEY COULD SWING FASTER.

ALSO, THE LIGHTER THE CLUBS, THE LESS THEY'RE GOING TO TAKE OUT OF YOU PHYSICALLY, WHICH CAN BE IMPORTANT TOWARD THE END OF A ROUND.

18
350 YDS
PAR 4

IN SELECTING GOLF CLUBS, BE PARTICULARLY METICULOUS ABOUT THE ANGLE BETWEEN CLUBHEAD AND HOSEL — IN OTHER WORDS, ABOUT THE WAY THEY LIE. SMALL ERRORS HERE CAN CAUSE BIG ONES ON THE COURSE.

JM

SHOULD THE TOE BE OFF THE GROUND AS YOU ADDRESS THE BALL, CHANCES ARE IT WILL BE THAT WAY AT IMPACT, CAUSING THE CLUBFACE TO CLOSE AND THE BALL TO HOOK AS THE HEEL TOUCHES DOWN FIRST.

CONVERSELY, A HEEL-UP CLUB AT ADDRESS WILL GENERALLY TOUCH DOWN TOE FIRST, CAUSING THE CLUBFACE TO OPEN AND THE BALL TO SLICE.

Go for Good Quality

YOU CAN'T "BUY" A GOLF GAME IN THE CLUBS YOU CHOOSE. BUT YOU CAN SAVE YOURSELF SHOTS BY SEEKING OUT GOOD-QUALITY EQUIPMENT... AND ESPECIALLY THE FINE WORKMANSHIP THAT PRODUCES COMPATABILITY OF EACH CLUB TO ALL THE OTHERS IN A SET.

IN WOODS, LOOK FOR SIMILARITY OF GRAIN PATTERN IN PERSIMMON OR LAMINATIONS IN BONDED-WOOD HEADS, AND ALSO FOR CONSISTENCY OF FACE BULGE AND ROLL. WITH IRONS, CHECK PARTICULARLY LIE, LEADING-EDGE CONFIGURATION, GRADATIONS OF OFFSET, AND GRIP THICKNESS.

WELL-MADE CLUBS WILL ALL LOOK LIKE MEMBERS OF THE SAME HAPPY FAMILY.

Join the Pros—Use a Glove

YOU HAVE NOTICED PERHAPS THAT ALMOST EVERY GOLFER ON THE PGA TOUR WEARS A GLOVE ON HIS LEADING HAND (WHICH IS USUALLY THE LEFT, OF COURSE).

THERE ARE TWO REASONS.

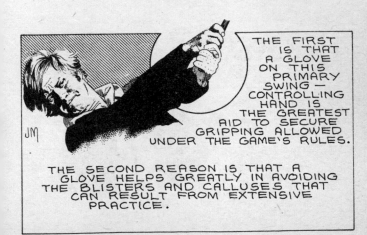

THE FIRST IS THAT A GLOVE ON THIS PRIMARY SWING—CONTROLLING HAND IS THE GREATEST AID TO SECURE GRIPPING ALLOWED UNDER THE GAME'S RULES.

THE SECOND REASON IS THAT A GLOVE HELPS GREATLY IN AVOIDING THE BLISTERS AND CALLUSES THAT CAN RESULT FROM EXTENSIVE PRACTICE.

Try to "Custom-Fit" Your Driver

BECAUSE THE CLUB IS SO IMPORTANT IN PLACING THE BALL IN PLAY, TOUR GOLFERS GO TO GREAT LENGTHS TO "CUSTOM FIT" THEIR DRIVERS TO THEIR INDIVIDUAL SWING STYLES. YOU MIGHT BENEFIT FROM SOME EXPERIMENT IN THIS DIRECTION IF YOU'RE A SERIOUS AND REASONABLY CAPABLE GOLFER.

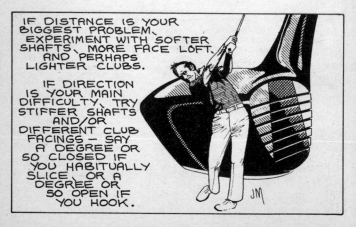

IF DISTANCE IS YOUR BIGGEST PROBLEM, EXPERIMENT WITH SOFTER SHAFTS, MORE FACE LOFT, AND PERHAPS LIGHTER CLUBS.

IF DIRECTION IS YOUR MAIN DIFFICULTY, TRY STIFFER SHAFTS AND/OR DIFFERENT CLUB FACINGS — SAY A DEGREE OR SO CLOSED IF YOU HABITUALLY SLICE, OR A DEGREE OR SO OPEN IF YOU HOOK.

Play the Ball You Can Really Handle

DON'T LET EGO DETERMINE THE COMPRESSION OF GOLF BALL YOU USE. A VERY POWERFUL SWING IS NECESSARY TO GET MAXIMUM DISTANCE FROM A HIGH COMPRESSION (100) BALL.

EVEN SOME OF THE TOUR PLAYERS PREFER A SLIGHTLY SOFTER BALL, ESPECIALLY IN COLD WEATHER.

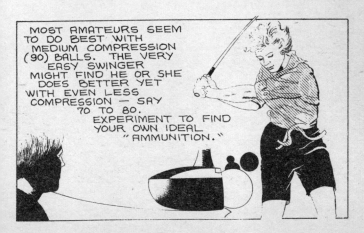

MOST AMATEURS SEEM TO DO BEST WITH MEDIUM COMPRESSION (90) BALLS. THE VERY EASY SWINGER MIGHT FIND HE OR SHE DOES BETTER YET WITH EVEN LESS COMPRESSION — SAY 70 TO 80. EXPERIMENT TO FIND YOUR OWN IDEAL "AMMUNITION."

PART TWO

The Swing
Step-by-Step

5

*Building a
Sound Grip*

Meet These Three Goals

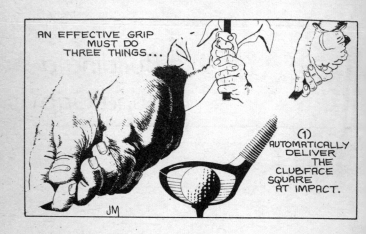

AN EFFECTIVE GRIP MUST DO THREE THINGS...

JM

(1) AUTOMATICALLY DELIVER THE CLUBFACE SQUARE AT IMPACT.

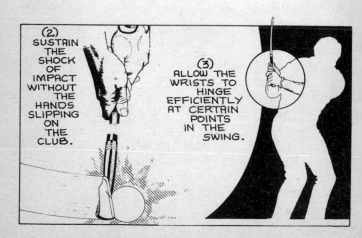

(2) SUSTAIN THE SHOCK OF IMPACT WITHOUT THE HANDS SLIPPING ON THE CLUB.

(3) ALLOW THE WRISTS TO HINGE EFFICIENTLY AT CERTAIN POINTS IN THE SWING.

Place Your Hands Naturally

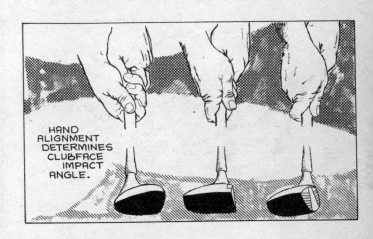

HAND ALIGNMENT DETERMINES CLUBFACE IMPACT ANGLE.

TO FIND YOUR MOST NATURAL GRIP, SIMPLY LET YOUR LEFT ARM HANG NORMALLY AT YOUR SIDE, THEN WRAP THE HAND SECURELY AROUND THE CLUB.

NEXT, EXTEND THE CLUB AND WRAP YOUR RIGHT HAND AROUND IT IN THE SAME ALIGNMENT IT HAD WHEN HANGING NATURALLY AT YOUR SIDE.

JM

Hold the Club like This

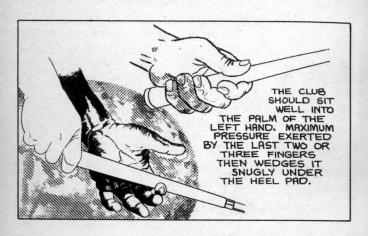

THE CLUB SHOULD SIT WELL INTO THE PALM OF THE LEFT HAND. MAXIMUM PRESSURE EXERTED BY THE LAST TWO OR THREE FINGERS THEN WEDGES IT SNUGLY UNDER THE HEEL PAD.

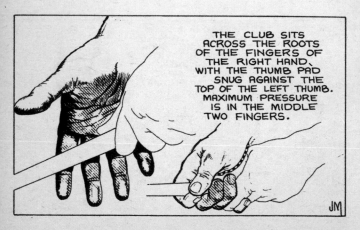

THE CLUB SITS ACROSS THE ROOTS OF THE FINGERS OF THE RIGHT HAND, WITH THE THUMB PAD SNUG AGAINST THE TOP OF THE LEFT THUMB. MAXIMUM PRESSURE IS IN THE MIDDLE TWO FINGERS.

Set Your Hands in Parallel

WHATEVER STYLE OF GRIP YOU CHOOSE — OVERLAPPING, INTERLOCKING OR 10-FINGER — KEEP IT AS **NATURAL** AS POSSIBLE. NATURALNESS COMES FROM SETTING THE HANDS PARALLEL WITH EACH OTHER RATHER THAN LOOKING IN OPPOSING DIRECTIONS.

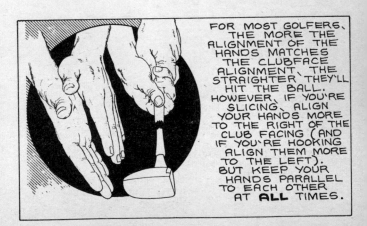

FOR MOST GOLFERS, THE MORE THE ALIGNMENT OF THE HANDS MATCHES THE CLUBFACE ALIGNMENT, THE STRAIGHTER THEY'LL HIT THE BALL. HOWEVER, IF YOU'RE SLICING, ALIGN YOUR HANDS MORE TO THE RIGHT OF THE CLUB FACING (AND IF YOU'RE HOOKING ALIGN THEM MORE TO THE LEFT). BUT KEEP YOUR HANDS PARALLEL TO EACH OTHER AT **ALL** TIMES.

Meld Your Hands Together

EFFICIENT WRIST HINGING AND RESISTANCE TO IMPACT SHOCK COME FROM LINKING THE HANDS AS A UNIT.

HAVING SMALL HANDS, I FAVOR THE <u>INTERLOCKING</u> GRIP.

MOST POPULAR MEANS OF UNIFYING THE HANDS IS THE OVERLAP, BUT GOLFERS WITH VERY WEAK HANDS MIGHT TRY THE 10 - FINGER GRIP.

WHATEVER STYLE YOU FAVOR, THE HANDS MUST BE AS <u>CLOSE TOGETHER</u> AS POSSIBLE.

Wedge *Shaft* into Left Palm

HOWEVER YOU GRIP — OVERLAP, INTERLOCK OR 10-FINGER STYLE — YOUR LEADING HAND NEEDS TO HANG ON VERY FIRMLY, FIRST TO GUIDE THE CLUB THROUGHOUT THE SWING, AND SECOND TO PROVIDE A BUTTRESS AGAINST THE HITTING ACTION OF THE TRAILING HAND.

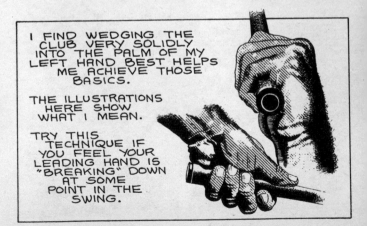

I FIND WEDGING THE CLUB VERY SOLIDLY INTO THE PALM OF MY LEFT HAND BEST HELPS ME ACHIEVE THOSE BASICS.

THE ILLUSTRATIONS HERE SHOW WHAT I MEAN.

TRY THIS TECHNIQUE IF YOU FEEL YOUR LEADING HAND IS "BREAKING" DOWN AT SOME POINT IN THE SWING.

Beware of Too "Strong" a Grip

MOST PEOPLE STARTING GOLF TEND TO TAKE A VERY "STRONG" GRIP ON THE CLUB, BECAUSE THEY INSTINCTIVELY FEEL THIS WILL GIVE THEM MORE POWER.

UNFORTUNATELY IT DOESN'T ALWAYS WORK THAT WAY.

JM

THE BETTER PLAYER DEVELOPS POWER WITH HIS **ENTIRE SWING**, NOT WITH JUST HIS HANDS AND WRISTS.

TOO STRONG A GRIP ACTUALLY INHIBITS THE FULL CLUBHEAD RELEASE NECESSARY FOR GOOD DISTANCE, SO WORK ON DEVELOPING A MORE "NEUTRAL" HOLD ON THE CLUB AS YOUR SWING SKILLS DEVELOP.

Maintain Consistent Pressure

TOO TIGHT A GRIP CAN DESTROY TEMPO AND RHYTHM BY FORCING YOU TO SWING JERKILY — ESPECIALLY DURING THE TAKEAWAY.

EVEN PRESSURE

HOLD THE CLUB LIGHTLY AT ADDRESS, FIRM UP YOUR HANDS SLIGHTLY JUST BEFORE YOU START BACK, THEN <u>MAINTAIN THE SAME PRESSURE</u> THROUGHOUT THE BACKSWING.

BIG THING TO AVOID IS GRABBING HARDER WITH EITHER HAND ONCE THE CLUB'S IN MOTION.

Test Your Grip like This

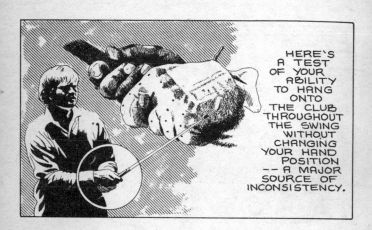

HERE'S A TEST OF YOUR ABILITY TO HANG ONTO THE CLUB THROUGHOUT THE SWING WITHOUT CHANGING YOUR HAND POSITION -- A MAJOR SOURCE OF INCONSISTENCY.

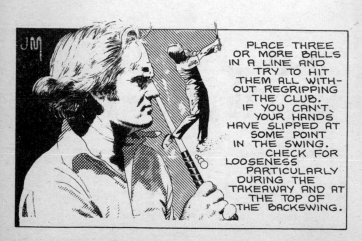

PLACE THREE OR MORE BALLS IN A LINE AND TRY TO HIT THEM ALL WITH-OUT REGRIPPING THE CLUB. IF YOU CAN'T, YOUR HANDS HAVE SLIPPED AT SOME POINT IN THE SWING. CHECK FOR LOOSENESS PARTICULARLY DURING THE TAKEAWAY AND AT THE TOP OF THE BACKSWING.

How to Aim
Accurately

Select a <u>Specific</u> Target

THE MORE SPECIFICALLY YOU SIGHT AND MENTALLY FOCUS ON A TARGET IN SETTING UP TO PLAY ANY SHOT, THE BETTER YOUR CHANCE OF HITTING WHERE YOU INTEND.

FOR THAT REASON, I ALWAYS TARGET TO A SPECIFIC POINT, RATHER THAN A VAGUE GREEN AREA, ON ALL APPROACH SHOTS. USUALLY THAT POINT IS THE PIN, BUT IF IT'S HIDDEN OR I CAN'T SHOOT DIRECTLY AT IT FOR SOME REASON, THEN I'LL SELECT A MOUND OR A TREE IN THE BACK-GROUND. MAKE A SPECIAL POINT OF DOING THIS WHENEVER YOUR APPROACH PLAY BECOMES LESS SHARP THAN YOU'D LIKE.

Use This 3-Point Aiming System

INCORRECT AIM AND ALIGNMENT LIES BEHIND PROBABLY 80 PER CENT OF GOLF'S MISDIRECTED SHOTS, ESPECIALLY AMONG HIGH HANDICAPPERS. HERE'S A ROUTINE THAT WILL HELP SOLVE THAT PROBLEM FOR YOU.

1. SELECT YOUR TARGET LINE FROM BEHIND THE BALL, AND USE A MARK ON THE GROUND A FEW FEET AHEAD OF IT AS A REFERENCE POINT. 2. SET THE CLUBFACE BEHIND THE BALL LOOKING SQUARELY AT YOUR MARK AND THUS DOWN YOUR TARGET LINE, BEFORE YOU FINALIZE YOUR GRIP AND STANCE. 3. ALIGN YOUR BODY PARALLEL TO THE TARGET LINE -- PARTICULARLY YOUR SHOULDERS.

Check Those Shoulders...

PLACING YOUR FEET PARALLEL TO THE TARGET LINE AT ADDRESS WILL HELP YOU SWING THE CLUB ALONG THAT LINE THROUGH IMPACT, BUT SETTING YOUR **SHOULDERS** SQUARE TO THE LINE WILL HELP YOU DO SO EVEN MORE.

REASON IS THAT THE CLUBHEAD PATH AT IMPACT USUALLY MATCHES THE ALIGNMENT OF THE SHOULDERS AT THAT MOMENT, AND THE ANGLE OF THE SHOULDERS AT IMPACT USUALLY MATCHES THEIR ANGLE AT ADDRESS. THUS IF YOU START WITH AN OPEN OR CLOSED SHOULDER LINE, YOU ALMOST GUARANTEE AN OUT-TO-IN OR IN-TO-OUT SWING PATH.

. . . and the Clubface

MOST GOLFERS INSTINCTIVELY LINE THEMSELVES UP PARALLEL TO WHERE THE CLUBFACE LOOKS AT ADDRESS.

MOST GOLFERS ALSO INSTINCTIVELY DELIVER THE CLUBHEAD TO THE BALL ON A PATH PARALLEL TO THEIR SHOULDER ALIGNMENT AT ADDRESS.

SO A SQUARE CLUBFACE AT ADDRESS ESTABLISHES YOUR BEST CHANCE OF SWINGING ALONG THE TARGET LINE AT IMPACT.

Never Neglect Your Alignment

CHECK YOUR ADDRESS ALIGNMENT FIRST ANY TIME YOU BEGIN TO MIS-DIRECT MORE SHOTS THAN NORMAL.

FAULTY AIMING CAUSES MORE BOGEYS THAN ANY OTHER SINGLE ERROR AMONG EXPERIENCED PLAYERS.

AND IT'S EASY TO SLIP INTO UNKNOWINGLY.

YOU'LL NOTICE AT TOUR EVENTS THAT THE PLAYERS ARE CONSTANTLY CHECKING THEIR OWN AND EACH OTHERS' SET-UPS.

HAVE A PRO OR A PAL CHECK YOURS PERIODICALLY, OR DO IT YOURSELF IN PRACTICE BY ALIGNING TO A CLUB LAID ON THE GROUND. REMEMBER THE GREATEST SWING IN THE WORLD WON'T SCORE IF IT'S MIS-AIMED.

7

Posture, Stance
and Ball Position

Don't Exaggerate Your Posture

KEY TO GOOD POSTURE IS TO AVOID EXAGGERATION.

FORCE ANYTHING AT ADDRESS AND INSTINCTIVELY IT WILL COME APART DURING YOUR SWING.

YOUR BASIC POSTURAL ADDRESS OBJECTIVE IS SIMPLY TO **MIRROR** YOUR IDEAL IMPACT POSITION. YOU'LL DO THAT MOST EFFECTIVELY BY BEING AS NATURAL AS POSSIBLE WITHIN GOOD SET-UP FUNDAMENTALS.

Set Shaft and Left Arm in Line

BY SETTING-UP WITH YOUR LEFT ARM AND CLUBSHAFT IN A STRAIGHT LINE FROM LEFT SHOULDER TO BALL, YOU'LL AUTOMATICALLY POSITION YOUR HANDS SLIGHTLY AHEAD OF THE CLUBHEAD — WHICH IS WHERE THEY SHOULD BE THROUGH IMPACT.

ANOTHER ADVANTAGE OF SETTING UP "IN LINE" LIKE THIS IS THAT IT AUTOMATICALLY PUTS THE RIGHT SIDE UNDER AND INSIDE THE LEFT SIDE. THAT'S ANOTHER IMPACT "MUST."

JM

Flex Your Knees Slightly

A SLIGHT FLEX IN BOTH KNEES IS CRITICAL TO GOOD LEG ACTION, SO BUILD IT INTO YOUR ADDRESS POSTURE.

BUT DON'T OVER-BEND YOUR KNEES, BECAUSE THAT LEADS TO SLOPPY LEG ACTION ON THE THROUGH-SWING.

SEEK THE FEELING OF FIRM RESILIENCE WITH JUST A LITTLE "GIVE" AT THE KNEES.

JM

Let Your Arms Hang Freely

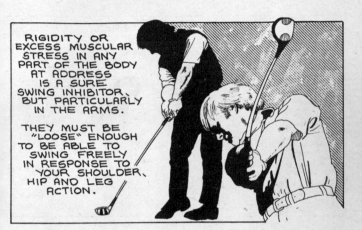

RIGIDITY OR EXCESS MUSCULAR STRESS IN ANY PART OF THE BODY AT ADDRESS IS A SURE SWING INHIBITOR, BUT PARTICULARLY IN THE ARMS.

THEY MUST BE "LOOSE" ENOUGH TO BE ABLE TO SWING FREELY IN RESPONSE TO YOUR SHOULDER, HIP AND LEG ACTION.

TO ENSURE THAT THEY ARE, LET THEM HANG FREELY FROM YOUR SHOULDERS IN A RELAXED AND NATURAL POSITION AS YOU SET UP TO THE BALL. AVOID ANY POSTURE THAT CREATES A FEELING OF TENSION, PARTICULARLY IN YOUR FOREARMS. IF THIS MEANS EASING YOUR GRIP PRESSURE A LITTLE, DO SO — IT WILL NATURALLY FIRM UP AS THE SWING PROCEEDS.

Be as Natural as You Can

WHERE SHOULD YOUR ELBOWS POINT AT ADDRESS?

THERE HAVE BEEN ALL SORTS OF THEORIES OVER THE YEARS — SOME OF THEM REQUIRING CONTORTION-ISTS SKILLS.

MY RECOMMENDATION IS THAT YOU TRY TO PLAY GOLF AS NATURALLY AS POSSIBLE, WHICH MEANS IN THIS RESPECT NOT CONSCIOUSLY TWIST-ING OR TURNING YOUR ELBOWS IN ANY PARTICULAR DIRECTION. UNFORCED IN ANY DIRECTION, THEY'LL PROBABLY BE IN THE SAME ALIGN-MENT AT ADDRESS AS WHEN YOUR ARMS HANG NATUR-ALLY AT YOUR SIDES, WHICH IS JUST FINE.

Strike a Balance in Stance Width

THE WIDTH OF YOUR STANCE HAS QUITE AN INFLUENCE ON THE QUALITY OF YOUR SWING.

IF IT'S TOO **WIDE**, TURNING FREELY AND FULLY BECOMES DIFFICULT.

IF IT'S TOO **NARROW**, YOU'LL LACK STABILITY AND BALANCE.

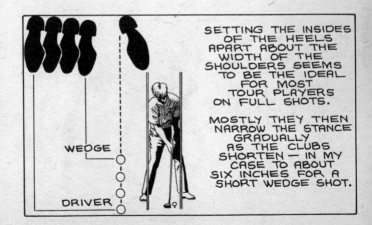

WEDGE

DRIVER

SETTING THE INSIDES OF THE HEELS APART ABOUT THE WIDTH OF THE SHOULDERS SEEMS TO BE THE IDEAL FOR MOST TOUR PLAYERS ON FULL SHOTS.

MOSTLY THEY THEN NARROW THE STANCE GRADUALLY AS THE CLUBS SHORTEN — IN MY CASE TO ABOUT SIX INCHES FOR A SHORT WEDGE SHOT.

Distribute Your Weight Evenly

SOME MODERN INSTRUCTORS SUGGEST SETTING MOST OF THE WEIGHT ON THE REAR FOOT AT ADDRESS, TO PRE-ESTABLISH THE WEIGHT TRANSFER AND ENSURE GOOD LEG ACTION INTO THE DOWNSWING.

I PREFER TO ACHIEVE THAT EFFECT BY DIVIDING MY WEIGHT EVENLY AT ADDRESS, THEN BRACING MYSELF BY **PUSHING** SLIGHTLY TOWARDS THE TARGET FROM THE <u>INSIDE</u> OF MY RIGHT FOOT.

THIS WAY THERE'S LESS CHANCE OF SWAYING THE UPPER BODY THAN WHEN MOST OF THE WEIGHT IS CONSCIOUSLY SET ON THE BACK FOOT.

JM

Angle Feet to Suit Swing Style

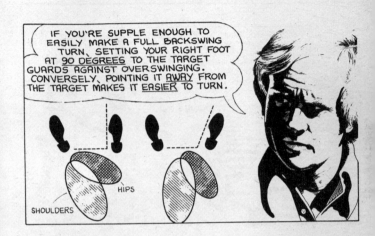

IF YOU'RE SUPPLE ENOUGH TO EASILY MAKE A FULL BACKSWING TURN, SETTING YOUR RIGHT FOOT AT 90 DEGREES TO THE TARGET GUARDS AGAINST OVERSWINGING. CONVERSELY, POINTING IT AWAY FROM THE TARGET MAKES IT EASIER TO TURN.

HIPS

SHOULDERS

ANGLING THE LEFT FOOT TOWARDS THE TARGET — AS I DO — ENCOURAGES FAST DOWNSWING HIP CLEARANCE.

BUT DON'T OVERDO THIS IF YOU HAVE A TENDENCY TO "SPIN OUT" WITH YOUR HIPS OR "COME OVER" THE BALL WITH YOUR SHOULDERS.

JM

Distance Yourself from Ball like This

TO FIND YOUR PROPER DISTANCE FROM THE BALL WITH ANY CLUB, STAND UPRIGHT BUT RELAXED, THEN FLEX YOUR KNEES SLIGHTLY AND SLUMP YOUR SHOULDERS DOWNWARD.

NOW BEND FROM THE WRIST UNTIL YOU CAN SET THE CLUB COMFORTABLY BEHIND THE BALL WITH YOUR ARMS HANGING ALMOST STRAIGHT DOWN.

YOUR LEFT ARM AND THE CLUB SHOULD DIP SLIGHTLY BENEATH AN IMAGINARY LINE RUNNING FROM YOUR LEFT SHOULDER TO THE BALL.

Position Ball at Bottom of Swing Arc

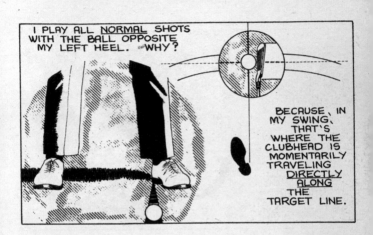

I PLAY ALL <u>NORMAL</u> SHOTS WITH THE BALL OPPOSITE MY LEFT HEEL. WHY?

BECAUSE, IN MY SWING, THAT'S WHERE THE CLUBHEAD IS MOMENTARILY TRAVELING <u>DIRECTLY ALONG</u> THE TARGET LINE.

IF I HAD THE BALL <u>BACK</u>, THE CLUBHEAD WOULD STILL BE COMING FROM <u>INSIDE</u>, AND I'D PUSH OR HOOK DEPENDING ON CLUBFACE ALIGNMENT.

IF I HAD THE BALL <u>FORWARD</u>, THE CLUBHEAD WOULD BE COMING FROM <u>OUTSIDE</u>, AND I'D PULL OR SLICE THE BALL.

EXPERIMENT TO FIND <u>YOUR</u> IDEAL BALL POSITION.

Center Clubface Behind Ball

CHECK PERIODICALLY THAT YOU ARE CENTERING THE CLUBFACE AGAINST THE BALL AT ADDRESS. MANY GOLFERS FAIL TO DO SO, WHICH CREATES EITHER TOE OR HEEL CONTACT OR NEEDLESS COMPENSATIONS AT SOME POINT IN THE SWING.

IF YOU FAIL TO MEET THE BALL SQUARELY AFTER HAVING ADDRESSED IT CORRECTLY, THERE IS A FLAW IN EITHER YOUR SET-UP OR YOUR SWING.

MOST OFTEN YOU'LL FIND THAT YOU'RE STANDING EITHER TOO FAR FROM OR TOO CLOSE TO THE BALL.

8

Starting Back

Stay in Motion to Avoid "Freezing"

STARTING BACK 1

A LOT OF JERKY SWINGS, AND VISITS TO THE WOODS, ARE THE RESULT OF "FREEZING" OVER THE BALL AT ADDRESS.

ALL GOOD GOLFERS STAY IN MOTION IN SOME PART OF THE BODY AS THEY GET READY TO SWING.

MOST POPULAR TENSION-PREVENTER IS THE WAGGLE, BUT I ALSO LIKE TO KEEP MY LEGS LOOSE BY SHIFTING MY WEIGHT SLIGHTLY FROM FOOT TO FOOT AS I GET SET TO SWING.

JM

Find Yourself a Swing "Trigger"

STARTING
BACK 2

EVERY GOLFER NEEDS AN EFFECTIVE SWING "TRIGGER," AND THERE ARE PLENTY TO CHOOSE FROM. FOR EXAMPLE, **GARY PLAYER** "KICKS IN" HIS RIGHT KNEE --

-- WHEREAS **JULIUS BOROS** GETS GOING OFF THE FINAL SHUFFLING OF HIS FEET INTO POSITION.

MOST POPULAR "TRIGGER" ON THE TOUR — AND THE ONE I FAVOR — IS THE FORWARD PRESS: A SLIGHT INCLINATION OF THE HANDS TOWARDS THE TARGET, FROM WHICH YOU "REBOUND" INTO THE TAKEAWAY.

STARTING
BACK
3

YOU CAN'T START A GOLF CLUB BACK TOO SLOWLY, PROVIDED YOU SWING RATHER THAN TAKE OR LIFT IT AWAY FROM THE BALL.

I TRY ON EVERY SHOT TO SWING INTO MOTION VERY DELIBERATELY — JUST FAST ENOUGH TO AVOID JERKINESS.

OBVIOUSLY THE MOTION SPEEDS UP AS THE BACKSWING PROGRESSES.

BUT THE SLOWER YOU CAN KEEP THOSE FIRST TWO OR THREE FEET, THE BETTER YOU'LL PLAY — ESPECIALLY WHEN YOU WANT DISTANCE.

78

Let Club Path Follow Body Turn

STARTING BACK 4

JACK, SHOULD I START THE CLUB BACK INSIDE OR ALONG THE TARGET LINE?

MOST TOUR PLAYERS— INCLUDING ME — START THE CLUB BACK ALONG THE TARGET LINE.

BUT IT ACTUALLY STAYS ON THAT LINE ONLY FOR A FOOT OR TWO, IF THAT.

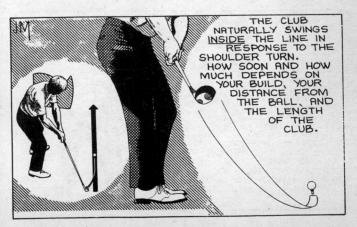

THE CLUB NATURALLY SWINGS INSIDE THE LINE IN RESPONSE TO THE SHOULDER TURN. HOW SOON AND HOW MUCH DEPENDS ON YOUR BUILD, YOUR DISTANCE FROM THE BALL, AND THE LENGTH OF THE CLUB.

Start Back in "One Piece"

STARTING BACK 5

I FAVOR A "ONE-PIECE" TAKEAWAY, WHICH MEANS KEEPING ALL MOVING PARTS OF THE BODY IN STEP WITH EACH OTHER DURING THE INITIAL BACKSWING MOTION.

A ONE-PIECE START-BACK SETS UP A WIDE SWING ARC, FORCES THE BODY TO TURN, PREVENTS "PICKING UP" THE CLUB WITH THE HANDS AND ARMS ONLY, AND PROMOTES A SMOOTH AND WELL-PACED OVERALL SWING TEMPO.

JM

Watch Out for Those Wrists!

STARTING BACK 6

OVER-ACTIVE HANDS AND WRISTS AT THE START OF THE SWING ARE RESPONSIBLE FOR A LOT OF GOLF'S FOUL BALLS.

MY LEFT ARM AND CLUB SHAFT RETAIN THE STRAIGHT-LINE RELATIONSHIP THEY FORM AT ADDRESS UNTIL MY HANDS REACH ABOUT HIP HEIGHT.

THEN THE WEIGHT OF THE RISING CLUBHEAD NATURALLY BEGINS TO COCK THE WRISTS WITHOUT ANY CONSCIOUS EFFORT ON MY PART.

Feel Left Shoulder Pushing Club Back

STARTING BACK 7

JACK, WHAT'S YOUR MAIN <u>FEELING</u> DURING THE EARLY PART OF THE BACKSWING?

THAT THE LEFT ARM AND CLUB ARE BEING **PUSHED** BACK BY MY LEFT SHOULDER AS IT BEGINS TO TURN <u>DOWN</u> AND AROUND UNDER MY CHIN.

A HELPFUL FEELING IS THAT YOUR LEFT ARM'S SWINGING MOTION NEVER GETS AHEAD OF YOUR LEFT SHOULDER'S <u>PUSHING</u> MOTION EARLY IN THE BACKSWING. THIS WILL ENCOURAGE YOU TO <u>TURN FULLY</u>, RATHER THAN JUST LIFTING THE CLUB WITH YOUR ARMS.

Don't Manipulate the Clubface

STARTING BACK 8

A SURE WAY TO GET ALL PRETZELED UP AT GOLF IS TO TRY TO FORCE THE CLUBFACE TO STAY "SQUARE" TO THE TARGET TOO LONG INTO THE BACK-SWING.

AS THE SHOULDERS TURN, THE CLUB-FACE WILL APPEAR TO "OPEN"— LOOK INCREASINGLY RIGHT OF TARGET. BUT WHEN YOU GO BACK IN "ONE PIECE," WITHOUT INDEPENDENT HAND/ARM MANIPULATION, IT WILL STILL BE CORRECTLY SQUARE TO THE ARC THE CLUB IS DESCRIBING.

JM

To the
Top

Know Your Options

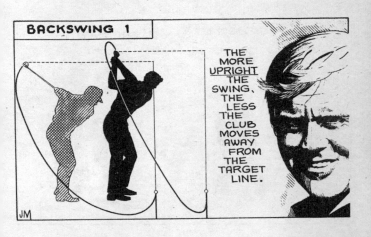

BACKSWING 1

THE MORE UPRIGHT THE SWING, THE LESS THE CLUB MOVES AWAY FROM THE TARGET LINE.

JM

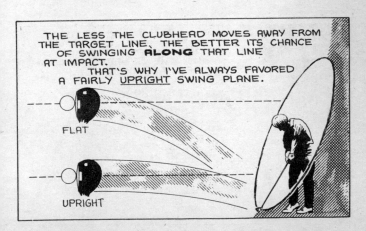

THE LESS THE CLUBHEAD MOVES AWAY FROM THE TARGET LINE, THE BETTER ITS CHANCE OF SWINGING **ALONG** THAT LINE AT IMPACT.

THAT'S WHY I'VE ALWAYS FAVORED A FAIRLY UPRIGHT SWING PLANE.

FLAT

UPRIGHT

Coil Shoulders, Swing Hands High

BACKSWING 2

DANGER OF BECOMING <u>TOO</u> UPRIGHT IS THAT THE CLUB WON'T STAY AT GROUND LEVEL LONG ENOUGH THROUGH IMPACT TO MEET THE BALL SOLIDLY.

JM

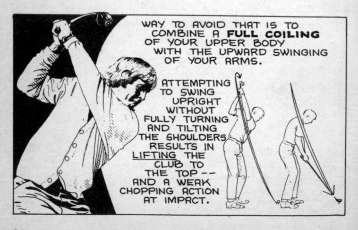

WAY TO AVOID THAT IS TO COMBINE A **FULL COILING** OF YOUR UPPER BODY WITH THE UPWARD SWINGING OF YOUR ARMS.

ATTEMPTING TO SWING UPRIGHT WITHOUT FULLY TURNING AND TILTING THE SHOULDERS RESULTS IN <u>LIFTING</u> THE CLUB TO THE TOP -- AND A WEAK CHOPPING ACTION AT IMPACT.

Extend Arms but Stay "Centered"

BACK-SWING 3

FIRST ESSENTIAL FOR A WIDE ARC IS <u>MAXIMUM EXTENSION</u> OF YOUR ARMS **AWAY** FROM YOU AS THEY SWING BACK AND UP, <u>WITHOUT SWAYING YOUR BODY</u>.

A <u>WIDE</u> SWING ARC IS ESSENTIAL TO GENERATE MAXIMUM CLUBHEAD SPEED THROUGH MAXIMUM LEVERAGE.

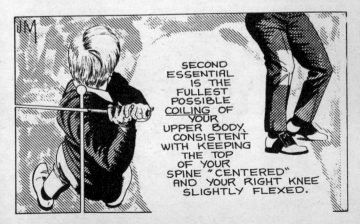

SECOND ESSENTIAL IS THE FULLEST POSSIBLE <u>COILING</u> OF YOUR UPPER BODY, CONSISTENT WITH KEEPING THE TOP OF YOUR SPINE "CENTERED" AND YOUR RIGHT KNEE SLIGHTLY FLEXED.

BACKSWING 4

MANY GOLFERS' POOR SWINGS ORIGINATE IN WEAK FOOT AND ANKLE ACTION.

BASICALLY, THE MORE YOU CAN SWING FROM THE <u>INSIDES</u> OF YOUR FEET, AND THE MORE OF YOUR FEET YOU CAN KEEP ON THE GROUND, THE BETTER YOU'LL PLAY.

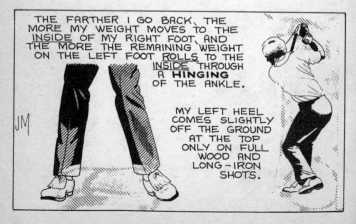

THE FARTHER I GO BACK, THE MORE MY WEIGHT MOVES TO THE <u>INSIDE</u> OF MY RIGHT FOOT, AND THE MORE THE REMAINING WEIGHT ON THE LEFT FOOT <u>ROLLS</u> TO THE <u>INSIDE</u> THROUGH A **HINGING** OF THE ANKLE.

MY LEFT HEEL COMES SLIGHTLY OFF THE GROUND AT THE TOP ONLY ON FULL WOOD AND LONG-IRON SHOTS.

JM

Anchor Swing with Flexed Right Knee

BACKSWING 5

YOUR RIGHT KNEE IS YOUR BACKSWING "ANCHOR".

KEEPING IT _FLEXED_ AND _RESILIENT_ IS THE KEY TO A STRONG WIND-UP AND PROPER DOWNSWING INITIATION.

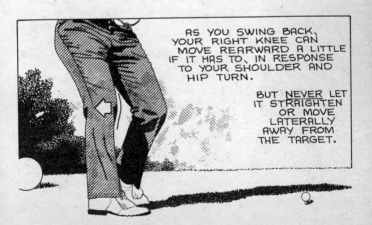

AS YOU SWING BACK, YOUR RIGHT KNEE CAN MOVE REARWARD A LITTLE IF IT HAS TO, IN RESPONSE TO YOUR SHOULDER AND HIP TURN.

BUT NEVER LET IT STRAIGHTEN OR MOVE LATERALLY AWAY FROM THE TARGET.

Let Left Knee Move Behind Ball

BACKSWING 6

TURNING FULLY IN THE SHOULDERS AND HIPS REQUIRES THAT YOUR LEFT KNEE FLEX <u>INWARD</u>, TOWARDS THE BALL, AS THE BACKSWING PROGRESSES.

BEWARE SIMPLY BENDING THE LEFT KNEE <u>FORWARD</u> BY LIFTING YOUR LEFT HEEL HIGH OFF THE GROUND.

PROPER LEG WORK CALLS FOR THE KNEE TO BE <u>PULLED</u> TOWARDS THE BALL BY THE FORCE OF YOUR BODY WIND-UP.

Beware Too Much Heel Lift

BACKSWING 7

LIFTING THE LEFT HEEL HIGH OFF THE GROUND IS A DANGEROUS MOVE, FOR TWO REASONS.

FIRST, THE RAISING ACTION MAY CAUSE AN INVOLUNTARY LIFTING OF THE ENTIRE BODY, WHICH WILL OBVIOUSLY DISTORT YOUR SWING ARC.

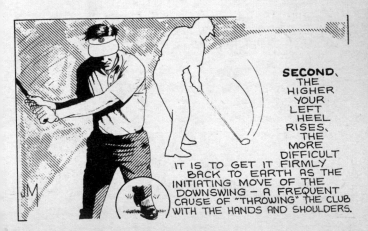

SECOND, THE HIGHER YOUR LEFT HEEL RISES, THE MORE DIFFICULT IT IS TO GET IT FIRMLY BACK TO EARTH AS THE INITIATING MOVE OF THE DOWNSWING — A FREQUENT CAUSE OF "THROWING" THE CLUB WITH THE HANDS AND SHOULDERS.

91

Don't Restrict Hip Turn...

BACKSWING 8

THERE'S A SCHOOL OF THOUGHT THAT SAYS THE HIPS SHOULD TURN VERY SLIGHTLY, IF AT ALL, ON THE BACKSWING.

I DON'T SUBSCRIBE TO IT, BECAUSE IF I DON'T LET MY HIPS TURN I CAN'T TURN MY SHOULDERS -- AND IF I DON'T TURN MY SHOULDERS I CAN'T GENERATE <u>LEVERAGE</u>.

THUS, GOING BACK, I ALLOW MY HIPS TO TURN <u>AS FAR AROUND AS THEY'LL GO</u> WITHOUT FORCING MY RIGHT LEG TO STRAIGHTEN OR COLLAPSE, OR MY WEIGHT TO MOVE TO THE OUTSIDE OF MY RIGHT FOOT.

YOU SHOULD, TOO.

BACKSWING 9

MODERN GOLFERS ALLOW THEIR HIPS TO TURN GOING BACK IN <u>RESPONSE</u> TO THE <u>PULL</u> OF THE SHOULDER TURN, NOT AS A CONSCIOUS OR INDEPENDENT ACT.

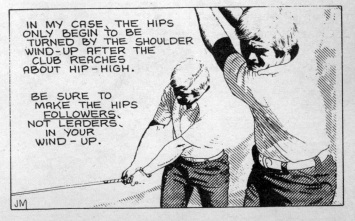

IN MY CASE, THE HIPS ONLY BEGIN TO BE TURNED BY THE SHOULDER WIND-UP AFTER THE CLUB REACHES ABOUT HIP-HIGH.

BE SURE TO MAKE THE HIPS <u>FOLLOWERS</u>, NOT LEADERS, IN YOUR WIND-UP.

JM

Make Your Spine Your Swing "Hub"

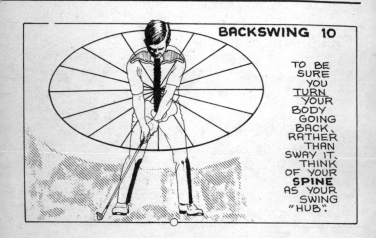

BACKSWING 10

TO BE SURE YOU <u>TURN</u> YOUR BODY GOING BACK, RATHER THAN SWAY IT, THINK OF YOUR **SPINE** AS YOUR SWING "HUB".

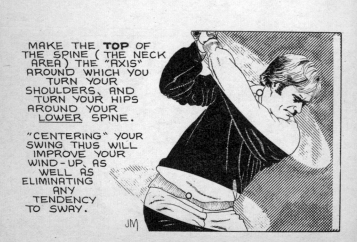

MAKE THE **TOP** OF THE SPINE (THE NECK AREA) THE "AXIS" AROUND WHICH YOU TURN YOUR SHOULDERS, AND TURN YOUR HIPS AROUND YOUR <u>LOWER</u> SPINE.

"CENTERING" YOUR SWING THUS WILL IMPROVE YOUR WIND-UP, AS WELL AS ELIMINATING ANY TENDENCY TO SWAY.

JM

Coil Your Shoulders as Fully as You Can

BACKSWING 11

FLAILING <u>AT</u> THE BALL WITH THE HANDS AND ARMS, INSTEAD OF **LEVERING** THE CLUB <u>THROUGH</u> IT VIA A FULL UPPER-BODY TURN, IS ONE OF GOLF'S COMMONEST FAULTS.

JM

CURE IS TO TURN YOUR SHOULDERS <u>AS FAR AROUND</u> AS THEY'LL GO SHORT OF FORCING YOUR RIGHT KNEE TO STIFFEN, YOUR WEIGHT TO MOVE TO THE OUTSIDE OF YOUR RIGHT FOOT, OR YOUR LEFT HEEL TO RISE MORE THAN ABOUT AN INCH OFF THE GROUND.

Practice These 3 "Feels"

BACKSWING 12

HERE ARE THREE PRACTICE-TEE THOUGHTS TO HELP YOU MAXIMIZE YOUR UPPER-BODY TURN.

FOR THE FIRST THIRD OF THE BACKSWING, DEVELOP THE FEELING THAT YOUR SHOULDERS ARE **PUSHING** YOUR ARMS BACK AND UP.

AS THE CLUB GETS HIP-HIGH, AND FOR THE NEXT THIRD OF THE BACKSWING, SWITCH TO A FEELING OF YOUR UP-SWINGING ARMS **PULLING** YOUR SHOULDERS AROUND.

DURING THE FINAL PART OF THE BACKSWING, CONCEN-TRATE ON THRUSTING YOUR HANDS AS HIGH AS THEY'LL GO BEHIND YOUR HEAD – REALLY "REACH FOR THE CLOUDS."

BACKSWING 13

GOLFERS OF OLD PLAYED WELL WITH BENT LEFT ARMS, BUT YOU DON'T SEE MANY ON TOUR TODAY.

REASON IS THE DIFFICULTY OF CONSISTENTLY REPRODUCING THE PROPER SWING PATH THROUGH IMPACT WHEN THE ARC-CONTROLLING ARM BENDS GOING BACK AND THEN STRAIGHTENS COMING DOWN.

A STRAIGHT-BUT-NOT-STIFF LEFT ARM IS MOST TOUR PROS' GOAL, INCLUDING ME.

KEY TO ATTAINING IT IS A FIRM LEFT-HAND GRIP, AND A ONE-PIECE MOVEMENT AWAY FROM THE BALL FROM THE LEFT SHOULDER TO THE CLUBHEAD.

97

Never Loosen Your Grip

BACKSWING 14

LOOSENING THE GRIP AT THE TOP OF THE BACKSWING IS A SURE ROUTE TO DISASTER.

MANY GOLFERS DO IT INVOLUNTARILY IN TRYING TO SWING LONGER WITHOUT MAKING A FULLER BODY TURN.

CHECK THIS POINT IF YOU ARE SPRAYING SHOTS.

CURE LIES IN ESTABLISHING A SECURE GRIP AT ADDRESS, AND SUSTAINING IT BY USING THE BODY TURN AS WELL AS THE HAND-AND-ARM SWING TO GET THE CLUB FULLY BACK.

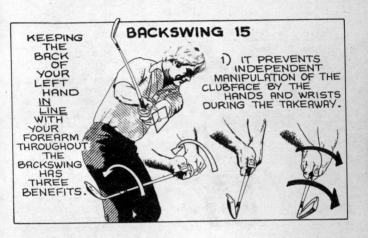

KEEPING THE BACK OF YOUR LEFT HAND IN LINE WITH YOUR FOREARM THROUGHOUT THE BACKSWING HAS THREE BENEFITS.

BACKSWING 15

1) IT PREVENTS INDEPENDENT MANIPULATION OF THE CLUBFACE BY THE HANDS AND WRISTS DURING THE TAKEAWAY.

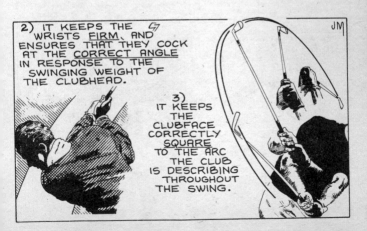

2) IT KEEPS THE WRISTS FIRM, AND ENSURES THAT THEY COCK AT THE CORRECT ANGLE IN RESPONSE TO THE SWINGING WEIGHT OF THE CLUBHEAD.

3) IT KEEPS THE CLUBFACE CORRECTLY SQUARE TO THE ARC THE CLUB IS DESCRIBING THROUGHOUT THE SWING.

JM

BACKSWING 16

SHOULD YOU "PAUSE" AT THE TOP? A FEW FINE GOLFERS HAVE — NOTABLY TWO-TIME U.S. OPEN CHAMPION **CARY MIDDLECOFF.**

I HAVE NO DISCERNIBLE PAUSE, BECAUSE MY LOWER BODY ACTUALLY BEGINS THE DOWNSWING JUST AS MY UPPER BODY IS COMPLETING THE BACKSWING.

HOWEVER, I DO HAVE A SENSE OF "WAITING" AT THE TOP IN MY HANDS, ARMS AND SHOULDERS UNTIL MY FEET, LEGS AND HIPS HAVE STARTED THE UNWINDING MOTION.

IT'S A FEELING YOU SHOULD CULTIVATE, TOO.

JM

Swing as "Long" as You Can

HOW FAR SHOULD I SWING BACK JACK?

BACK-SWING 17

AS FAR AS YOU CAN WITHOUT STIFFENING YOUR RIGHT KNEE, FORCING YOUR WEIGHT TO THE OUTSIDE OF YOUR RIGHT FOOT, LIFTING YOUR LEFT HEEL HIGH, BENDING YOUR LEFT ARM, OR LOOSENING YOUR GRIP.

JM

WITHIN THOSE CONDITIONS, THE LONGER YOUR SWING THE BETTER YOU'LL PLAY -- AND THE LONGER YOU'LL GO ON PLAYING WELL.

YOU DON'T SEE MANY SENIOR CHAMPIONS WITH SHORT SWINGS — AS WITNESS SAM SNEAD.

10

Down and Through

Look for Downswing Fault
in Backswing

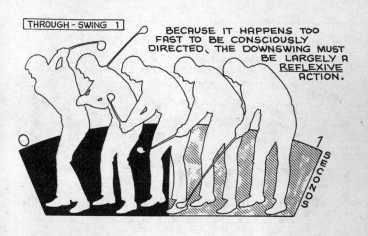

THROUGH - SWING 1

BECAUSE IT HAPPENS TOO FAST TO BE CONSCIOUSLY DIRECTED, THE DOWNSWING MUST BE LARGELY A <u>REFLEXIVE</u> ACTION.

1 SECONDS

SO, IF YOU'RE FAULTY COMING DOWN, THE FIRST PLACE TO LOOK FOR THE PROBLEM IS IN HOW YOU GO BACK.

BUILD A GOOD BACKSWING AND YOU'LL AUTOMATICALLY DEVELOP A GOOD THROUGH - SWING PATTERN.

103

Reverse "Halves" Coming Down

HERE'S THE BASIC FACTOR TO ALWAYS REMEMBER ABOUT GOLF'S BACKWARD AND FORWARD MOTIONS.

GOING BACK, YOUR LOWER BODY WORKS IN RESPONSE TO THE COILING OF YOUR UPPER BODY. EXACTLY THE REVERSE MUST HAPPEN COMING DOWN — YOUR UPPER BODY MUST RESPOND ONLY TO THE UNCOILING OF YOUR LOWER BODY.

THAT'S FUNDAMENTAL WHATEVER YOUR PERSONAL SWING STYLE.

Maximize Your Leverage

THROUGH-SWING 3

VERY FEW GOLFERS (GOOD ONES) ACTUALLY PAUSE — HALT ALL MOTION — AT THE TOP OF THE BACKSWING.

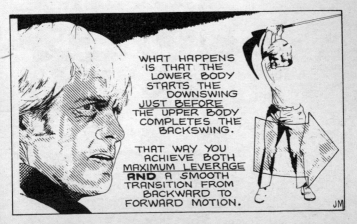

WHAT HAPPENS IS THAT THE LOWER BODY STARTS THE DOWNSWING JUST BEFORE THE UPPER BODY COMPLETES THE BACKSWING.

THAT WAY YOU ACHIEVE BOTH MAXIMUM LEVERAGE AND A SMOOTH TRANSITION FROM BACKWARD TO FORWARD MOTION.

JM

Swing Down from Feet Up

THROUGH-SWING 4

MOST GOLFERS WOULD IMPROVE IMMENSELY BY LEARNING TO START DOWN WITH THEIR <u>FEET</u> RATHER THAN THEIR HANDS.

GET THE FEELING OF YOUR LEFT HEEL REPLANTING SOLIDLY AS YOU PUSH HARD OFF THE <u>INSIDE</u> OF YOUR RIGHT FOOT.

DO THAT BEFORE ANYTHING UP TOP UNWINDS AND YOU'RE 90 PER CENT OF THE WAY TO PROPER LOWER-BODY ACTION.

Never Hurry Your Shoulders

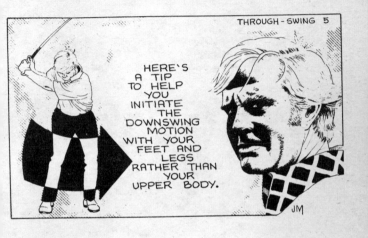

THROUGH-SWING 5

HERE'S A TIP TO HELP YOU INITIATE THE DOWNSWING MOTION WITH YOUR FEET AND LEGS RATHER THAN YOUR UPPER BODY.

JM

SLOW

AS YOU START BACK TO THE BALL, TRY TO KEEP THE UPWARD MOVEMENT OF YOUR LEFT SHOULDER AS <u>SLOW</u> AS POSSIBLE.

THE SLOWER THIS HAPPENS, THE MORE TIME YOUR LEGS HAVE TO MOVE TARGETWARDS BEFORE YOUR SHOULDERS UNWIND.

Flex—and Use—Those Knees

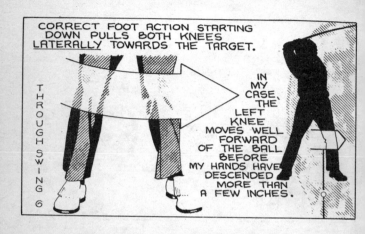

CORRECT FOOT ACTION STARTING DOWN PULLS BOTH KNEES __LATERALLY__ TOWARDS THE TARGET.

THROUGH SWING 6

IN MY CASE, THE LEFT KNEE MOVES WELL FORWARD OF THE BALL BEFORE MY HANDS HAVE DESCENDED MORE THAN A FEW INCHES.

KEY TO ACHIEVING AND SUSTAINING THIS STRONG LEG ACTION IS TO KEEP __BOTH__ KNEES FLEXED THROUGH IMPACT.

STIFFENING THE LEFT LEG TOO FAST IS A FREQUENT CAUSE OF SPINNING THE SHOULDERS OVER THE BALL.

S-t-r-e-t-c-h That Left Side

THROUGH - SWING 7

MANY GOLFERS HAVE A PROBLEM COMBINING A FLEXED LEFT KNEE THROUGH IMPACT WITH A FIRM LEFT SIDE.

FEELING TO STRIVE FOR IS ONE OF STRETCHING FROM YOUR LEFT FOOT TO YOUR LEFT SHOULDER WITHOUT STRAIGHTENING YOUR LEFT LEG — OR RAISING YOUR HEAD — UNTIL THE BALL HAS BEEN STRUCK.

THE BETTER SHAPE YOUR LEGS ARE IN, THE EASIER THIS BECOMES.

Don't Think About Wrist Action

THROUGH SWING 8

A GOOD TRANSITION FROM BACKSWING TO DOWNSWING ELIMINATES ANY NEED FOR DELIBERATE WRIST-COCKING.

NEARING THE TOP, THE SWINGING WEIGHT OF THE CLUBHEAD WILL NATURALLY BEGIN TO HINGE YOUR WRISTS.

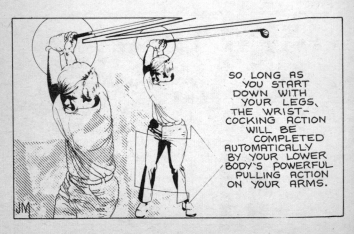

SO LONG AS YOU START DOWN WITH YOUR LEGS, THE WRIST-COCKING ACTION WILL BE COMPLETED AUTOMATICALLY BY YOUR LOWER BODY'S POWERFUL PULLING ACTION ON YOUR ARMS.

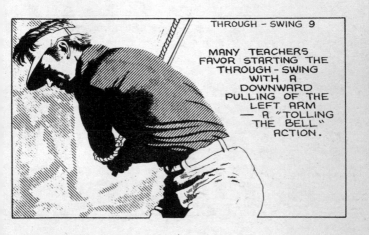

THROUGH – SWING 9

MANY TEACHERS FAVOR STARTING THE THROUGH – SWING WITH A DOWNWARD PULLING OF THE LEFT ARM — A "TOLLING THE BELL" ACTION.

THAT'S FINE SO LONG AS YOUR LEGS WORK IN HARNESS WITH YOUR ARM SWING.

IF YOUR LEGS DON'T MOVE JUST A LITTLE AHEAD OF YOUR ARMS, CHANCES ARE YOUR ARMS WILL PULL YOUR SHOULDERS FORWARD 'OVER' THE BALL.

JM

Avoid These 3 Errors

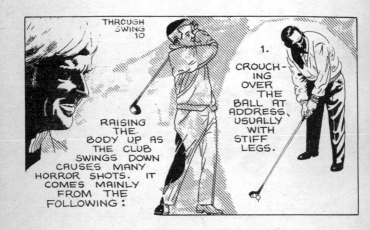

THROUGH SWING 10

1. CROUCHING OVER THE BALL AT ADDRESS, USUALLY WITH STIFF LEGS.

RAISING THE BODY UP AS THE CLUB SWINGS DOWN CAUSES MANY HORROR SHOTS. IT COMES MAINLY FROM THE FOLLOWING:

JM

2. THROWING THE CLUB FROM THE TOP WITH THE HANDS AND WRISTS.

3. FAILING TO START DOWN WITH THE FEET AND KNEES, WHICH KEEPS THE WEIGHT ON THE RIGHT SIDE AND STIFFENS THE LEGS.

Let Hips Follow Knees...

THROUGH-SWING 11

ONCE YOUR KNEES HAVE MOVED TARGETWARDS COMING DOWN, YOUR HIPS <u>MUST</u> TURN TOWARDS THE TARGET TO CLEAR A PATH FOR YOUR ARMS TO SWING PAST YOUR BODY.

KEY HERE IS NEVER TO LET YOUR HIPS TURN AHEAD OF YOUR TARGETWARDS KNEE MOTION.

LETTING YOUR HIPS UNCOIL AHEAD OF YOUR LEG ACTION — "SPINNING OUT," THE PROS CALL IT — IS A SURE WAY TO SWING "OVER" THE BALL.

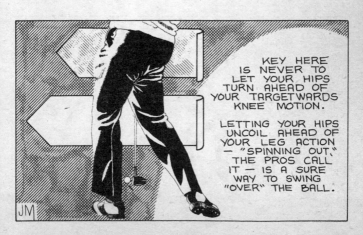

...but Keep Lower-Body Action _Smooth_

THROUGH SWING 12

IN TRYING TO IMPROVE YOUR LOWER-BODY ACTION, BE CAREFUL NOT TO OVER-DO YOUR LEG/HIP MOTION TO THE POINT WHERE YOU LURCH YOUR ENTIRE BODY FORWARD.

JM

KEY IS TO THRUST YOUR KNEES _SMOOTHLY_ TOWARDS THE TARGET, AND YOUR HIPS GRADUALLY AROUND TO FACE IT, WHILE KEEPING YOUR HEAD WELL _BEHIND_ THE BALL.

Prefer "Left-Side" Thoughts

THROUGH-SWING 13

I BASICALLY CONTROL THE SWING WITH MY <u>LEFT SIDE</u>, BUT IF THINGS AREN'T GOING WELL I'LL TRY EMPHASIZING RIGHT-SIDE ACTION.

FOR EXAMPLE, MY PREFERRED THOUGHT COMING DOWN IS " MOVE THE LEFT SHOULDER UP AND THE LEFT HIP AROUND."

BUT IF THAT DOESN'T SEEM TO BE WORKING, I'LL TRY "MOVE THE <u>RIGHT</u> SHOULDER <u>DOWN</u> AND THE RIGHT HIP AROUND."

BALANCING OUT SWING "FEELS" THUS MIGHT HELP YOU PLAY BETTER.

JM

Work Lower Body—Then Release!

THROUGH - SWING 14

JOE, YOU'RE LETTING ALL THAT STUFF ABOUT HITTING "LATE" WITH THE HANDS AND WRISTS PREVENT YOU FROM RELEASING THE CLUBHEAD THROUGH THE BALL!

AS LONG AS YOU START DOWN WITH YOUR LOWER BODY AND KEEP IT MOVING AHEAD OF YOUR UPPER HALF, YOU CAN'T HIT TOO "EARLY" WITH YOUR HANDS AND WRISTS.

SO GET THOSE LEGS GOING, AND THEN LET THAT CLUBHEAD **FLY**!

Meld Hip and Hand/Wrist Action

THROUGH - SWING 15

IF YOUR BASIC SWING PATTERN IS SOUND BUT YOU START TO SLICE SHOTS, CHANCES ARE YOUR HIP ACTION IS GETTING AHEAD OF YOUR HAND/WRIST ACTION.

EITHER SLOWING DOWN YOUR HIP UNWIND OR SPEEDING UP YOUR CLUBHEAD RELEASE SHOULD STRAIGHTEN YOU OUT.

IF THE PROBLEM'S A HOOK, CHANCES ARE THAT YOUR HANDS/WRISTS ARE RELEASING THE CLUB BEFORE YOU'VE ACHIEVED SUFFICIENT HIP CLEARANCE.

ANSWER HERE IS TO EITHER SPEED UP YOUR HIP ACTION OR HOLD BACK A LITTLE ON YOUR CLUBHEAD RELEASE.

Check for This Sign of "Spinning"

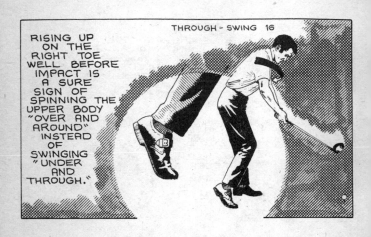

THROUGH - SWING 16

RISING UP ON THE RIGHT TOE WELL BEFORE IMPACT IS A SURE SIGN OF SPINNING THE UPPER BODY "OVER AND AROUND" INSTEAD OF SWINGING "UNDER AND THROUGH."

ONE WAY TO CURE THIS UGLY MOVE IS TO PRACTICE HITTING SHOTS WHILE KEEPING THE RIGHT HEEL ANCHORED AND THE RIGHT KNEE FACING THE BALL.

IT'LL BE A WHOLE NEW FEEL, SO START WITH THE SHORT IRONS AND WORK UP.

Let Right Arm Straighten

THROUGH SWING 17

IN MOST GOOD GOLF SWINGS THE RIGHT ELBOW STAYS SLIGHTLY BENT, AND POINTING TOWARDS THE RIGHT SIDE, RIGHT UP UNTIL IMPACT.

ONCE THE BALL IS STRUCK, HOWEVER, A QUICKLY STRAIGHTENING AND EXTENDING RIGHT ARM IS A SIGN OF FULL CLUBHEAD RELEASE. FEELING I LIKE AT THAT POINT IS OF ALMOST BEING ABLE TO REACH OUT AND RETRIEVE THE FLYING BALL WITH MY RIGHT HAND.

Chase Ball with Clubface

THROUGH SWING 18

GREATER ARM EXTENSION THROUGH THE BALL WOULD HELP MANY GOLFERS WITH DIRECTIONAL PROBLEMS.

JM

FEELING I OFTEN SEEK WHEN I NEED MAXIMUM ACCURACY IS THAT OF KEEPING THE CLUBFACE ON THE BALL AS LONG AS POSSIBLE AFTER IMPACT.

FIRM WRISTS AND STAYING WELL <u>DOWN</u> <u>AND BACK</u> ON THE SHOT ARE ESSENTIAL TO PROMOTE IT.

Think "Acceleration"

SCIENTISTS SAY IT'S IMPOSSIBLE TO ACTUALLY KEEP ON ACCELERATING THE CLUBHEAD THROUGH THE BALL — THAT IT ALWAYS REACHES MAXIMUM SPEED <u>BEFORE</u> IMPACT.

THROUGH - SWING 19

NEVERTHELESS, I THINK IT PAYS TO HAVE THE FEELING OF **TRYING** TO ACCELERATE THROUGH THE BALL AND BEYOND. DANGER IS THAT, IF YOU DO NOT <u>THINK</u> ACCELERATION, YOU'LL PROBABLY DECELERATE BEFORE IMPACT.

ACCELERATION!

THROUGH SWING 20

BIG DOWN-SWING FAULT OF HIGH HANDICAP GOLFERS IS HITTING <u>AT</u> THE BALL INSTEAD OF SWINGING THE CLUBHEAD FREELY <u>THROUGH</u> IT.

JM

ONE WAY TO OVERCOME THIS IS TO PRACTICE WHILE IMAGINING THE BALL SIMPLY ISN'T THERE.

IF THAT DOESN'T WORK, FOCUSING MENTALLY ON ACHIEVING A SPECIFIC FOLLOW-THROUGH PATTERN OR "FEEL" WILL REDUCE YOUR BALL CONSCIOUSNESS.

11

Tempo, Rhythm and Timing

TIMING IS A WORD FOR THE WAY ALL YOUR SWING MOTIONS MELD TOGETHER.

WHEN THE MELD PRODUCES MAXIMUM SQUARENESS OF CLUBFACE AND CLUBHEAD SPEED AT IMPACT, YOUR TIMING IS PERFECT.

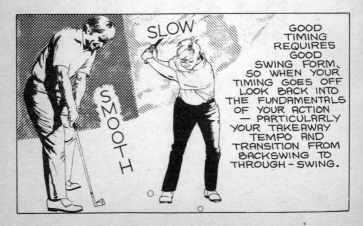

SLOW

SMOOTH

GOOD TIMING REQUIRES GOOD SWING FORM, SO WHEN YOUR TIMING GOES OFF LOOK BACK INTO THE FUNDAMENTALS OF YOUR ACTION — PARTICULARLY YOUR TAKEAWAY TEMPO AND TRANSITION FROM BACKSWING TO THROUGH-SWING.

Swing Rhythmically Within Natural Tempo

YOUR TEMPO, OR SPEED OF SWING, IS LARGELY DETERMINED BY YOUR PERSONALITY.

DELIBERATE PEOPLE NATURALLY TEND TO SWING SLOWLY, HYPERACTIVE PEOPLE QUICKLY.

RATHER THAN TAMPER WITH WHAT COMES NATURALLY, STRIVE TO SWING <u>RHYTHMICALLY</u> WHATEVER YOUR PACE.

RHYTHM IS THE QUALITY WITH WHICH YOU MELD ALL THE MOVING PARTS OF THE SWING, AND THE SMOOTHER IT IS THE BETTER YOUR TIMING WILL BE.

Use Bigger Muscles for Smoother Action

A SLOWER SWING ISN'T NECESSARILY GOING TO IMPROVE YOUR GAME, BUT A **SMOOTHER TEMPO** ALMOST ALWAYS WILL.

IT'S MY EXPERIENCE THAT THE BIGGER THE MUSCLES YOU USE TO PROPEL THE CLUB, THE MORE FLUIDLY AND SMOOTHLY YOU CAN SWING IT.

SO, IN WORKING ON YOUR TEMPO, BE WARY OF OVER-DOING THE HAND AND WRIST ACTION AT THE EXPENSE OF YOUR BACK AND LEGS.

USE A FULL UPPER BODY TURN TO GET THE CLUB BACK, AND A STRONG LEG DRIVE TO GET IT STARTED DOWN — AND ONLY **THEN** BRING THE HANDS AND WRISTS INTO MAXIMUM PLAY.

126

Work on Rhythm When Timing Is Off

BEWARE OF TRYING TO CHANGE YOUR OVERALL SPEED OF SWING, BECAUSE THIS ALMOST CERTAINLY IS A PRODUCT OF YOUR PERSONALITY, AND AS SUCH PRETTY DIFFICULT TO CHANGE EFFECTIVELY.

INSTEAD, WHEN YOU FEEL YOUR TIMING IS "OFF," CONCENTRATE ON THE **RHYTHM** OF YOUR ACTION RATHER THAN ITS OVERALL PACE.

WHETHER YOU NATURALLY SWING FAST OR SLOW, STRIVE FOR **SMOOTHNESS** OF MOTION FROM TAKEAWAY TO COMPLETION OF FOLLOW-THROUGH.

ALSO, THINKING OF SWINGING THE CLUBHEAD **THROUGH** THE BALL, NOT **AT IT**, IS OFTEN HELPFUL IN IMPROVING TIMING.

Try for Same Tempo with All Clubs

BEGINNERS AT GOLF OFTEN SEEM TO THINK THEY NEED A DIFFERENT SWING FOR EVERY CLUB IN THE BAG. THAT ISN'T TRUE — AND ESPECIALLY NOT IN TERMS OF TEMPO.

HIGH-SPEED FILMS OF ME HAVE SHOWN THAT WHEN PLAYING WELL, MY SWING POSITIONS ARE THE SAME WHETHER SWINGING A ONE-IRON OR AN 8-IRON.... WHICH MEANS MY TEMPO IS PRETTY MUCH IDENTICAL.

THAT'S A GOAL I THINK EVERY GOLFER SHOULD STRIVE FOR.

Make Driver Swing Your Tempo Model

OBVIOUSLY THE SHORTER THE CLUB, THE SHORTER THE ELAPSED TIME OF THE SWING.

BUT YOU SHOULDN'T <u>FEEL</u> THAT YOU SWING A WEDGE ANY FASTER THAN YOU SWING A DRIVER.

WHEN I'M PLAYING WELL, I FEEL THAT THE <u>PACE</u> OF MY SWING IS EXACTLY THE SAME WITH EVERY CLUB IN THE BAG — EVEN THE PUTTER. AND THE IDEAL PACE IN MY CASE IS THE DRIVER SWING — THE SLOWEST.

Try This to Smooth Out Takeaway

I'M ONE OF A SMALL NUMBER OF TOUR PLAYERS WHO NEVER GROUND THE CLUB AT ADDRESS.

THE TECHNIQUE BEGAN IN MY CASE AS A GUARD AGAINST ACCIDENTALLY MOVING THE BALL OR STUBBING THE CLUB STARTING BACK. BUT ITS BIGGEST VALUE HAS LONG BEEN ITS SMOOTHING EFFECT ON MY TAKEAWAY.

IT TAKES A WHILE TO GET USED TO STARTING BACK FROM AN UNGROUNDED POSITION. BUT IT'S A CERTAIN WAY TO SMOOTH OUT A JERKY TAKEAWAY, AND A BIG HELP IN BUILDING A ONE-PIECE BACKSWING.

BEGIN WITH THE SHORT IRONS AND WORK UP IF YOU DECIDE TO GIVE IT A TRY.

SMOOTH

Beware of a Dead Halt at Top

IS "PAUSE AT THE TOP" A GOOD THOUGHT?

NOT, IN MY VIEW, IF IT CAUSES YOU TO LITERALLY COME TO A DEAD STOP BEFORE YOU START DOWN AGAIN, BECAUSE THAT'S A SURE WAY TO WRECK YOUR TEMPO AND MOMENTUM — NOT TO MENTION YOUR BALANCE.

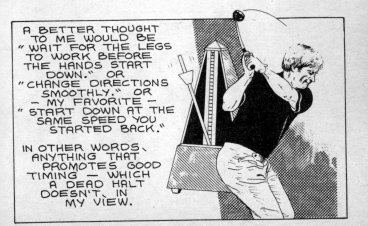

A BETTER THOUGHT TO ME WOULD BE "WAIT FOR THE LEGS TO WORK BEFORE THE HANDS START DOWN." OR "CHANGE DIRECTIONS SMOOTHLY." OR — MY FAVORITE — "START DOWN AT THE SAME SPEED YOU STARTED BACK."

IN OTHER WORDS, ANYTHING THAT PROMOTES GOOD TIMING — WHICH A DEAD HALT DOESN'T, IN MY VIEW.

Sense Swinging Weight of Clubhead

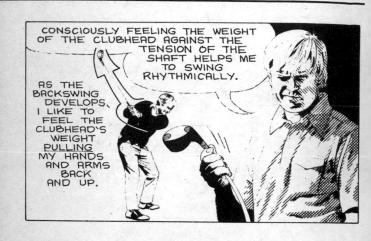

CONSCIOUSLY FEELING THE WEIGHT OF THE CLUBHEAD AGAINST THE TENSION OF THE SHAFT HELPS ME TO SWING RHYTHMICALLY.

AS THE BACKSWING DEVELOPS, I LIKE TO FEEL THE CLUBHEAD'S WEIGHT <u>PULLING</u> MY HANDS AND ARMS BACK AND UP.

STARTING DOWN, I LIKE TO FEEL THE CLUBHEAD WEIGHT <u>LAGGING</u> BACK — RESISTING — AS MY LOWER-BODY ACTION PULLS MY ARMS DOWN.

WHEN I CAN WAIT FOR THESE "FEELS," I'M USUALLY GIVING MYSELF TIME TO MOVE EVERYTHING IN PROPER SEQUENCE, AND THUS MY TEMPO IS EXCELLENT.

12

Power!

Never Hit for Distance Only

IS DISTANCE AS BIG A GOLFING ASSET AS MOST PLAYERS SEEM TO THINK IT IS ??

ONLY IF YOU CAN HIT LONG **AND STRAIGHT** — AND ONLY THEN IF YOU USE LENGTH INTELLIGENTLY.

FOR EXAMPLE, YOUR PRINCIPAL GOAL ON A DRIVE IS TO PLACE THE BALL IN THE EASIEST POSSIBLE POSITION FOR THE NEXT SHOT. NEARNESS TO THE HOLE ISN'T THE BEST POSITION IF THE BALL ENDS UP IN A LAKE OR A FOREST — OR EVEN ON A SHARP DOWNHILL LIE. SO DRIVE FOR THE BEST APPROACH ANGLES COMBINED WITH THE MOST LEVEL LIES — **NOT** FOR SHEER YARDAGE ALONE.

Beware the "Steering" Tendency

AS A KID I WAS TAUGHT BY JACK GROUT TO HIT HARD FIRST AND DEVELOP ACCURACY LATER.

MANY GOLFERS LACK DISTANCE BECAUSE THEY'VE HABITUALIZED "BABYING" OR "STEERING" THE BALL STRAIGHT.

JM

INCREASED BODY TURN AND ARM EXTENSION WILL LET YOU TAKE A BIGGER CUT AT IT.

BUT TRY FIRST ON A DRIVING RANGE. AND KEEP YOUR HEAD STILL AND YOUR TEMPO **SMOOTH**.

Stay a Little Within Yourself

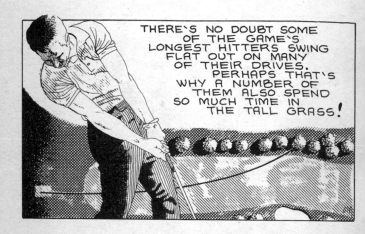

THERE'S NO DOUBT SOME OF THE GAME'S LONGEST HITTERS SWING FLAT OUT ON MANY OF THEIR DRIVES. PERHAPS THAT'S WHY A NUMBER OF THEM ALSO SPEND SO MUCH TIME IN THE TALL GRASS!

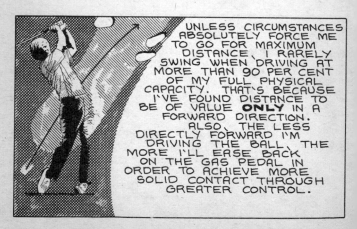

UNLESS CIRCUMSTANCES ABSOLUTELY FORCE ME TO GO FOR MAXIMUM DISTANCE, I RARELY SWING WHEN DRIVING AT MORE THAN 90 PER CENT OF MY FULL PHYSICAL CAPACITY. THAT'S BECAUSE I'VE FOUND DISTANCE TO BE OF VALUE **ONLY** IN A FORWARD DIRECTION. ALSO, THE LESS DIRECTLY FORWARD I'M DRIVING THE BALL, THE MORE I'LL EASE BACK ON THE GAS PEDAL IN ORDER TO ACHIEVE MORE SOLID CONTACT THROUGH GREATER CONTROL.

THE WOMEN PROFESSIONALS ARE LIVING PROOF THAT STRENGTH ALONE DOESN'T PRODUCE DISTANCE IN GOLF.

QUITE A NUMBER OF THE **LPGA** PROFESSIONALS DRIVE THE BALL FARTHER THAN MOST MALE CLUB GOLFERS.

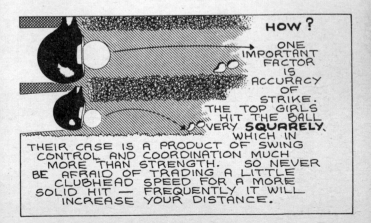

HOW?

ONE IMPORTANT FACTOR IS ACCURACY OF STRIKE. THE TOP GIRLS HIT THE BALL VERY **SQUARELY**, WHICH IN THEIR CASE IS A PRODUCT OF SWING CONTROL AND COORDINATION MUCH MORE THAN STRENGTH. SO NEVER BE AFRAID OF TRADING A LITTLE CLUBHEAD SPEED FOR A MORE SOLID HIT — FREQUENTLY IT WILL INCREASE YOUR DISTANCE.

THERE ARE BASICALLY TWO WAYS TO GET DISTANCE! ONE IS VIA A LONG, HIGH, FLOATING CARRY --- WHICH IS THE WAY I FAVOR BECAUSE IT OFFERS THE GREATEST CONTROL. BUT IT TAKES A CERTAIN AMOUNT OF STRENGTH AND AN UPRIGHT SWING PLANE.

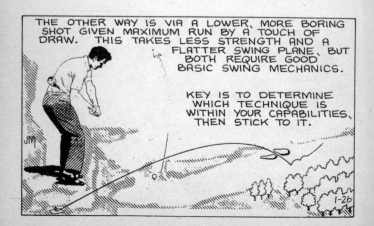

THE OTHER WAY IS VIA A LOWER, MORE BORING SHOT GIVEN MAXIMUM RUN BY A TOUCH OF DRAW. THIS TAKES LESS STRENGTH AND A FLATTER SWING PLANE, BUT BOTH REQUIRE GOOD BASIC SWING MECHANICS.

KEY IS TO DETERMINE WHICH TECHNIQUE IS WITHIN YOUR CAPABILITIES, THEN STICK TO IT.

1-26

Don't Cramp Your Style

TOO MANY GOLFERS CRAMP OR OVER-FLATTEN THEIR SWINGS BY TRYING TO AVOID A "FLYING" RIGHT ELBOW.

YOU CAN'T GET FULL ARM EXTENSION — AND THUS MAXIMUM DISTANCE-PRODUCING LEVERAGE — IF YOU OVER-CONSTRICT YOUR RIGHT ELBOW.

MY RIGHT ARM MOVES WELL AWAY FROM AND BEHIND MY BODY ON THE BACKSWING, BUT IT'S NOT "FLYING."

TO DO THAT IT WOULD HAVE TO POINT OUTWARD — BEHIND ME — WHEREAS IT ACTUALLY POINTS TOWARD THE GROUND.

SO, LONG AS YOURS DOES THE SAME, IT WON'T BE "FLYING" EITHER.

LOSING DISTANCE AS THOSE BIRTHDAYS KEEP COMING ALONG FASTER AND FASTER ??

TRY LETTING YOUR HIPS TURN A LITTLE MORE FULLY GOING BACK IN RESPONSE TO YOUR ARM SWING AND SHOULDER WIND-UP.

IT'S TRUE THAT MANY OF THE YOUNGER OR MORE FLEXIBLE TOUR PLAYERS DON'T TURN THEIR HIPS MUCH -- BUT IT'S ALSO TRUE THAT **BOBBY JONES** WON HIS 13 MAJORS TURNING HIS HIPS ALMOST AS MUCH AS HIS SHOULDERS.

IN MY VIEW, A LOT OF HIP TURN IS BETTER THAN NONE — ESPECIALLY FOR SENIORS AND STOCKY PLAYERS.

MOST AMATEURS WHEN TRYING FOR EXTRA DISTANCE INSTINCTIVELY TRY TO HIT HARDER WITH THEIR HANDS AND ARMS FROM THE TOP OF THE BACKSWING. IT'S A SURE WAY TO BOTH DIMINISH CLUBHEAD SPEED AND DISTORT CLUBFACE ALIGNMENT.

MY PRIMARY THOUGHT IN GOING FOR A BIG ONE IS A FASTER HIP UNWIND THROUGHOUT THE DOWNSWING. SO LONG AS YOU CAN KEEP THE ACTION SMOOTH AND FLUID, THE FASTER YOU UNCOIL YOUR HIPS THE GREATER THE LEVERAGE YOU CREATE, AND THUS THE FASTER YOU'LL WHIP THE CLUBHEAD THROUGH THE BALL.

CHECK THE HEIGHT YOU TEE THE BALL IF YOUR DRIVES ARE STOPPING SHORTER THAN YOU'D LIKE.

TEEING THE BALL LOW ENCOURAGES HITTING DOWN ON IT, WHICH INCREASES BACKSPIN, WHICH <u>DECREASES</u> ROLL.

JM

TEEING THE BALL SO THAT ITS CENTER IS ABOUT EVEN WITH THE TOP EDGE OF THE DRIVER WILL ENCOURAGE YOU TO <u>SWEEP</u> THE CLUBHEAD THROUGH ON A MORE LEVEL PATH AT IMPACT. THAT'LL GIVE YOU BOTH MAXIMUM CARRY <u>AND</u> ROLL.

Extend That Arc!

no. 7
572 YDS
PAR 5

USUAL RESULT OF AN ATTEMPT TO DRIVE FARTHER IS A VICE-LIKE GRIP, AN EXCESSIVE PIVOT, A SWAYING HEAD, A BENT LEFT ARM, AND A SHOULDER-SPINNING LUNGE AT THE BALL COMING DOWN.

NEXT TIME YOU NEED A BIG ONE, FORGET TRYING TO 'FORCE' THE SHOT.

INSTEAD, STAY WITH YOUR BASIC SWING MOVES AND TEMPO, BUT SIMPLY TRY TO <u>EXTEND THE ARC</u> BY GETTING YOUR ARMS HIGHER AT THE TOP.

DON'T START DOWN UNTIL YOU'VE FELT YOUR HANDS REACH **ABOVE** YOUR SHOULDERS.

CONSIDER YOUR RIGHT FOOT PLACEMENT IF YOU'RE HAVING TROUBLE MAKING A GOOD, FULL BODY TURN.

CURRENT PRO TOUR FASHION IS TO SET THE REAR FOOT AT 90 DEGREES TO THE TARGET LINE, BUT THAT'S TOO RESTRICTIVE FOR MANY SENIOR AND LESS SUPPLE GOLFERS.

THE FARTHER THE RIGHT FOOT POINTS AWAY FROM THE TARGET, THE FARTHER THE HIPS CAN BE ROTATED, AND THE FARTHER THE HIPS CAN BE ROTATED, THE MORE FULLY THE SHOULDERS CAN BE COILED.

SO POINT YOUR FOOT FOR POWER, NOT FOR APPEARANCES.

WHEN I'M REALLY GOING FOR A BIG HIT, I MAKE A SLIGHT STANCE ADJUSTMENT THAT HELPS ME SPEED UP MY LEG THRUST AND HIP CLEARANCE.

15th HOLE
PAR 5 520 YDS.
AUGUSTA NATIONAL

BY TURNING MY LEFT FOOT TARGETWARDS A LITTLE MORE, I GIVE MYSELF A RUNNING START ON SHIFTING MY HIPS OUT OF THE WAY FASTER ON THE FORWARD SWING.

IF YOU TRY THIS, BE SURE TO START DOWN WITH YOUR LEGS — OTHERWISE YOU RISK SPINNING OUT WITH YOUR SHOULDERS!

JM

145

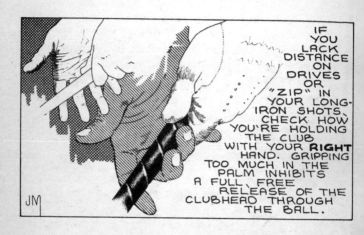

IF YOU LACK DISTANCE ON DRIVES OR "ZIP" IN YOUR LONG-IRON SHOTS, CHECK HOW YOU'RE HOLDING THE CLUB WITH YOUR **RIGHT** HAND. GRIPPING TOO MUCH IN THE PALM INHIBITS A FULL, FREE RELEASE OF THE CLUBHEAD THROUGH THE BALL.

TRY TO THROW A BALL HELD IN THE PALM OF YOUR HAND AND YOU WON'T MOVE IT VERY FAR.

GRIP THE BALL TOWARDS THE END OF YOUR FINGERS AND YOU CAN REALLY SLING IT.

LONG-HITTING AT GOLF REQUIRES THE SAME SORT OF SLINGING ACTION THROUGH IMPACT.

Let Clubhead Release Fully

FOR THE CLUB-HEAD TO BE FULLY RELEASED, THE RIGHT HAND AND WRIST MUST ROLL OVER THE LEFT SOMETIME BEYOND IMPACT.

JM

BLOCKING OR OVER-DELAYING THAT ACTION IN AN EFFORT TO HOLD THE CLUBFACE SQUARE TO THE TARGET TOO LONG IS ONE REASON MANY GOLFERS LACK REAL "ZIP" IN THEIR SHOTS.

THE KEY IS TO LET THE FOREARMS ROTATE NATURALLY INTO THE FOLLOW-THROUGH, WITHOUT (A) THE LEFT WRIST BREAKING DOWN BY CUPPING INWARD (B).

A.

B.

PART THREE

Special Factors and Situations

13

The Lower-Body
Action

Allow Your Weight to Shift

THE MORE YOU CAN KEEP THE WEIGHT ON THE **INSIDES** OF YOUR FEET DURING THE SWING, THE MORE "CENTERED" YOUR BODY WILL BE AND THE LESS CHANCE YOU'LL HAVE OF SWAYING OFF THE BALL.

80%

20%

AT THE TOP I FEEL I HAVE ABOUT 80 PER CENT OF MY WEIGHT ON THE INSIDE OF MY RIGHT FOOT AND THE REST ON THE INSIDE OF MY LEFT.

AT **IMPACT**, THESE PROPORTIONS ARE REVERSED, WITH ALMOST ALL THE WEIGHT EVENTUALLY GOING OVER TO THE OUTSIDE EDGE OF THE LEFT FOOT AS THE FOLLOW-THROUGH PROGRESSES.

Practice "Rolling" with Heels Down

THE MORE YOU CAN ROLL RATHER THAN "DANCE" ON YOUR FEET, THE BETTER GOLF YOU'LL PLAY.

SOME OF THE BEST PRACTICE I EVER SPENT AS A YOUNGSTER WAS HITTING SHOTS WITHOUT ALLOWING MY HEELS TO LEAVE THE GROUND.

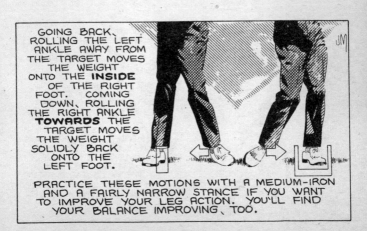

GOING BACK, ROLLING THE LEFT ANKLE AWAY FROM THE TARGET MOVES THE WEIGHT ONTO THE **INSIDE** OF THE RIGHT FOOT. COMING DOWN, ROLLING THE RIGHT ANKLE **TOWARDS** THE TARGET MOVES THE WEIGHT SOLIDLY BACK ONTO THE LEFT FOOT.

PRACTICE THESE MOTIONS WITH A MEDIUM-IRON AND A FAIRLY NARROW STANCE IF YOU WANT TO IMPROVE YOUR LEG ACTION. YOU'LL FIND YOUR BALANCE IMPROVING, TOO.

Don't Deliberately Lift Left Heel

WHETHER YOUR LEFT HEEL LIFTS ON A FULL SWING DEPENDS ON YOUR SUPPLENESS. IF IT <u>HAS</u> TO COME OFF THE GROUND TO FACILITATE A FULL BODY TURN — AS IN MY CASE WITH THE LONGER CLUBS — THEN LET IT.

IF YOU CAN MAKE A GOOD WIND-UP WITHOUT RAISING THE LEFT HEEL, THEN YOU'VE GOT <u>TWO</u> ADVANTAGES OVER THOSE WHO MUST LET IT LIFT.

ONE IS THAT YOU'LL GET BACK FASTER ONTO YOUR LEFT SIDE COMING DOWN.

THE OTHER IS THAT YOUR LEFT FOOT WILL NOT MOVE OUT OF POSITION AS YOU SHIFT YOUR WEIGHT —— AS SOMETIMES HAPPENS IN MY CASE.

Check Your Knee Flex

HOW MUCH SHOULD YOUR KNEES BEND OR FLEX AT ADDRESS AND THROUGHOUT THE SWING?

THE EXACT DEGREE DEPENDS ON YOUR BUILD AND SWING STYLE, BUT YOU SHOULD WORK WITHIN CERTAIN LIMITS.

SETTING-UP AND SWINGING WITH THE LEGS TOO STRAIGHT OR STIFF BREEDS TENSION AND RESTRICTS TURN BY LOCKING THE BODY.

TOO MUCH SAG IN THE KNEES UNDERMINES SOLID ANCHORING AND LOWER BODY RESILIENCE.

SO TRY TO FIND A HAPPY MEDIUM, COMBINING COMFORT WITH A SENSE OF SPRINGY 'READINESS' IN THE LEGS.

Work on Your Right-Leg Action

SWAYING AND/OR STIFFENING THE RIGHT LEG GOING BACK CAUSES MUCH HEARTACHE FOR WEEKEND GOLFERS. REASON IS THAT SUCH MOVES PREVENT BOTH PROPER <u>WEIGHT - SHIFTING</u> AND <u>HIP CLEARANCE</u> COMING DOWN.

FLEX YOUR RIGHT KNEE SLIGHTLY AT ADDRESS AND KEEP IT THAT WAY THROUGHOUT THE BACKSWING. DEVELOP THE FEELING OF COILING AROUND A <u>FIXED BUT FLEXED</u> RIGHT KNEE.

PRACTICING WITH A GOLF BALL UNDER THE OUTER EDGE OF THE FOOT WILL QUICKLY TEACH YOU THE PROPER RIGHT LEG ACTION.

Learn Proper Weight Shift like This

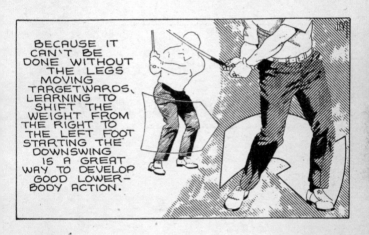

BECAUSE IT CAN'T BE DONE WITHOUT THE LEGS MOVING TARGETWARDS, LEARNING TO SHIFT THE WEIGHT FROM THE RIGHT TO THE LEFT FOOT STARTING THE DOWNSWING IS A GREAT WAY TO DEVELOP GOOD LOWER-BODY ACTION.

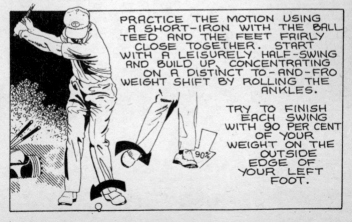

PRACTICE THE MOTION USING A SHORT-IRON WITH THE BALL TEED AND THE FEET FAIRLY CLOSE TOGETHER. START WITH A LEISURELY HALF-SWING AND BUILD UP, CONCENTRATING ON A DISTINCT TO-AND-FRO WEIGHT SHIFT BY ROLLING THE ANKLES.

TRY TO FINISH EACH SWING WITH 90 PER CENT OF YOUR WEIGHT ON THE OUTSIDE EDGE OF YOUR LEFT FOOT.

14

The Role of the
Hands and Wrists

WHAT'S THE ROLE OF THE HANDS AND WRISTS IN GOLF?

THAT'S BEEN A SUBJECT OF GREAT DEBATE EVER SINCE THE GAME BEGAN, AND PROBABLY WILL BE AS LONG AS IT'S PLAYED.

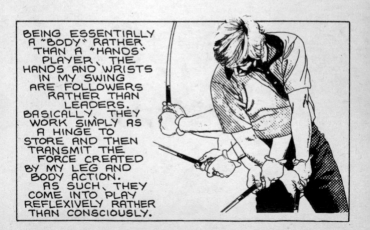

BEING ESSENTIALLY A "BODY" RATHER THAN A "HANDS" PLAYER, THE HANDS AND WRISTS IN MY SWING ARE FOLLOWERS RATHER THAN LEADERS. BASICALLY, THEY WORK SIMPLY AS A HINGE TO STORE AND THEN TRANSMIT THE FORCE CREATED BY MY LEG AND BODY ACTION. AS SUCH, THEY COME INTO PLAY REFLEXIVELY RATHER THAN CONSCIOUSLY.

159

Allow Your Wrists to Cock Reflexively

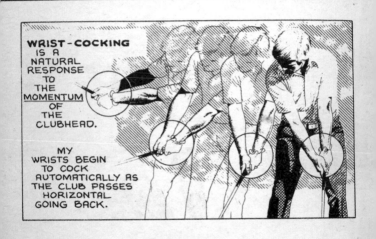

WRIST-COCKING IS A NATURAL RESPONSE TO THE MOMENTUM OF THE CLUBHEAD.

MY WRISTS BEGIN TO COCK AUTOMATICALLY AS THE CLUB PASSES HORIZONTAL GOING BACK.

THE FARTHER BACK I GET, THE MORE MY WRISTS COCK IN RESPONSE TO THE SWINGING WEIGHT OF THE CLUBHEAD.

YOU'LL NEVER HAVE TO THINK ABOUT YOUR WRISTS IF YOU GRIP THE CLUB FIRMLY AND MAKE A FULL BODY TURN AND ARM SWING — THEY'LL COCK REFLEXIVELY.

JM

"Reach for the Sky" with Your Hands

THE HIGHER THE HANDS AT THE TOP, THE BETTER THE GOLF SWING AS I SEE IT.

IF YOU HAVE DIFFICULTY CREATING THE FULL BODY TURN AND ARM EXTENSION THAT HIGH HANDS SIGNIFY, HERE'S A TIP THAT MIGHT HELP YOU.

GOING BACK, STRIVE FOR THE FEELING THAT YOUR LEFT ARM AND THE CLUB SHAFT REMAIN IN A STRAIGHT LINE UNTIL THE WEIGHT OF THE SWINGING CLUBHEAD CAUSES YOUR WRISTS TO HINGE INVOLUNTARILY. SWING SMOOTHLY AND DELIBERATELY AND YOU'LL FIND IT MUCH EASIER TO "REACH FOR THE SKY" WITH THIS ONE-PIECE TAKEAWAY FEELING.

Guide with Left, Hit with Right

IS THERE SUCH A THING AS "TOO MUCH RIGHT HAND" IN GOLF?

NOT IN MY VIEW!

IF THE RIGHT HAND OVERPOWERS THE LEFT, IT'S BECAUSE THE LEFT HAS BEEN USED IMPROPERLY.

JM

THE LEFT HAND SHOULD CERTAINLY BE THE DOMINANT FACTOR IN GUIDING AND DIRECTING THE CLUB TO THE BALL. BUT IF IT DOES THAT CORRECTLY, YOU CAN – AND SHOULD – HIT AS HARD AS POSSIBLE WITH THE RIGHT HAND.

IN OTHER WORDS, YOU CAN USE **BOTH** HANDS TO THE UTMOST, SO LONG AS YOU USE THEM <u>PROPERLY</u>.

"HANDS" PLAYERS SEEM TO HAVE MORE TIMING PROBLEMS THAN "BODY" GOLFERS, PERHAPS BECAUSE SMALL MUSCLES OPERATE FASTER AND MORE SPONTANEOUSLY THAN BIG ONES.

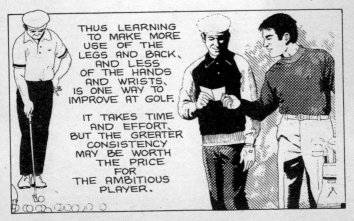

THUS LEARNING TO MAKE MORE USE OF THE LEGS AND BACK, AND LESS OF THE HANDS AND WRISTS, IS ONE WAY TO IMPROVE AT GOLF.

IT TAKES TIME AND EFFORT, BUT THE GREATER CONSISTENCY MAY BE WORTH THE PRICE FOR THE AMBITIOUS PLAYER.

163

15

The All-Important Head

Copy the Masters—Stay Steady

THERE ARE A LOT OF WAYS TO PLAY GOOD GOLF, BUT THEY ALL HAVE ONE THING IN COMMON: A **STEADY HEAD**.

JM

KEEPING YOUR HEAD STEADY ISN'T THE SAME THING AS "KEEPING YOUR EYE ON THE BALL" — I CAN SWAY MY HEAD TWO FEET AND STILL SEE THE BALL.

THE KEY TO HEAD STEADINESS IS NOT ALLOWING THE BACK OF YOUR NECK TO MOVE UP, DOWN OR SIDEWAYS AT ANY POINT FROM TAKEAWAY TO IMPACT.

THAT TAKES DISCIPLINE — AND <u>PRACTICE</u>.

Avoid These 3 Shot-Wreckers

YOUR HEAD IS YOUR SWING FULCRUM.
IF IT MOVES SUBSTANTIALLY ONE OR ALL OF THE FOLLOWING WILL HAPPEN:

1. YOUR ARC AND PLANE WILL CHANGE.

2. YOUR EYES WILL RELATE INCORRECTLY TO YOUR TARGET LINE.

3. YOU'LL LOSE BALANCE.

JM

LEARNING TO KEEP THE HEAD STEADY IS ONE OF GOLF'S TOUGHEST CHALLENGES, BUT IT'S AN ABSOLUTE **MUST** IF YOU WISH TO PLAY THE GAME WELL. THE ONLY ANSWERS ARE WILLPOWER AND PRACTICE — SUFFICIENT PRACTICE TO AUTOMATE SWINGING **AROUND** YOUR HEAD, NOT WITH IT.

YOU'LL NEVER HIT THE BALL _SOLIDLY_ _FORWARD_ IF YOUR HEAD ISN'T SOLIDLY _BEHIND_ IT AT IMPACT. MY HEAD AT THAT POINT STAYS BEHIND A VERTICAL LINE DRAWN UP FROM THE BALL.

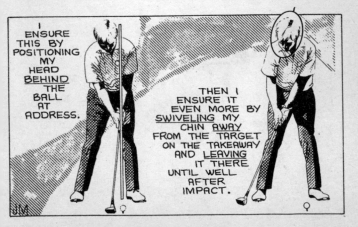

I ENSURE THIS BY POSITIONING MY HEAD _BEHIND_ THE BALL AT ADDRESS.

THEN I ENSURE IT EVEN MORE BY _SWIVELING_ MY CHIN _AWAY_ FROM THE TARGET ON THE TAKEAWAY AND _LEAVING_ IT THERE UNTIL WELL AFTER IMPACT.

A STEADY HEAD IS THE NO. 1 FUNDAMENTAL OF GOLF, BUT IT <u>CAN</u> BE OVERDONE.

IN FACT, TRYING TO LOOK AT THE BALL POSITION TOO LONG AFTER IMPACT ON A FULL SWING CAN ACTUALLY CAUSE YOUR HEAD TO BE FORCED UPWARD BY THE UNWINDING MOTION OF YOUR BODY.

TRICK IS TO LET YOUR HEAD <u>SWIVEL</u> SLOWLY SIDEWAYS, <u>WITHOUT LIFTING</u>, AS THE BODY SWINGS UNDER IT INTO THE FOLLOW-THROUGH.

THAT WAY YOU CAN STILL KEEP YOUR HEAD <u>DOWN AND CENTERED</u> WITHOUT INHIBITING YOUR ARM AND BODY ACTION THROUGH THE BALL.

Beware of Up-and-Down Movement

ALTHOUGH EVEN THE BEST GOLFERS' HEADS DO MOVE A LITTLE DURING THE SWING, I BELIEVE **THINKING** OF KEEPING THE HEAD IN ONE PLACE, AT LEAST UNTIL IMPACT, DEFINITELY HELPS IN STRIKING THE BALL SOLIDLY.

AVOID UP-AND-DOWN HEAD MOVEMENT AS WELL AS SIDE-TO-SIDE. IF YOUR HEAD GOES DOWN ON THE BACKSWING AND UP ON THE THROUGH-SWING, YOU'LL TOP A LOT OF SHOTS.

IF THE REVERSE HAPPENS — UP IN THE BACKSWING AND DOWN IN THE THROUGH-SWING — YOU'LL HIT A LOT OF SHOTS "FAT" (GROUND BEFORE BALL).

Check Your Head Action the Hard Way

THE BEST WAY TO CHECK HEAD MOVEMENT IS TO HAVE SOMEONE WATCH YOUR HEAD AGAINST A BACKGROUND POINT.

IF YOU HAVE TROUBLE KEEPING THE TOP HALF STEADY, HIT A FEW SHOTS WHILE SOMEONE GRABS YOUR HAIR.

IT MAY BRING TEARS TO YOUR EYES, BUT IT'LL GET THE MESSAGE ACROSS FASTER THAN ANYTHING I KNOW!

SWIVELING THE CHIN TO MAKE ROOM FOR MAXIMUM SHOULDER TURN — AS I DO — IS O.K. SO LONG AS THE BACK OF YOUR NECK REMAINS STEADY.

JM

16

Angled
Lies

YOU DON'T LIKE HILLY LIES?

WELL, I'VE HAD MY HOT MOMENTS ABOUT THEM TOO, BUT I'VE ALWAYS COOLED DOWN WHEN I THOUGHT HOW DULL THE GAME WOULD BE IF THE WORLD WAS DEAD FLAT.

TREAT ANGLED LIES AS AN INTEGRAL CHALLENGE OF THE GAME AND YOU'LL APPROACH THEM A LOT MORE POSITIVELY. YOU'LL PLAY THEM EVEN MORE POSITIVELY YET IF YOU INCLUDE A VARIETY OF THEM IN YOUR PRACTICE SESSIONS AS I DO — ESPECIALLY ON CHIPPING AND PITCHING.

WHAT IS THE MOST IMPORTANT ADJUSTMENT TO MAKE WHEN FACED WITH AN UPHILL OR DOWNHILL LIE?

MY ANSWER WOULD BE TO TAKE SPECIAL CARE OVER <u>CLUB SELECTION.</u>

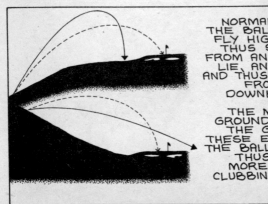

NORMALLY HIT, THE BALL WILL FLY HIGHER AND THUS SHORTER FROM AN UPHILL LIE, AND LOWER AND THUS FARTHER FROM A DOWNHILL LIE.

THE MORE THE GROUND SLOPES, THE GREATER THESE EFFECTS ON THE BALL'S FLIGHT, THUS THE MORE CRITICAL CLUBBING BECOMES.

Weight Back When Ground Slopes Down

A SEVERE DOWNHILL LIE IS TOUGH BECAUSE IT PRESENTS A BALANCE PROBLEM AS WELL AS REQUIRING SWING ADJUSTMENTS. TO TAKE CARE OF THE BALANCE FACTOR, OPEN YOUR STANCE AND SET MOST OF YOUR WEIGHT ON YOUR BACK FOOT.

TAKE A MORE LOFTED CLUB, TOO, SO THAT YOU CAN GET ADEQUATE HEIGHT WITHOUT PRESSING TOO HARD.

REGARDING SWING ADJUSTMENTS, PLAY THE BALL MORE TOWARD YOUR RIGHT FOOT AND OPEN THE CLUBFACE A LITTLE TO OFFSET A PULLING TENDENCY.

THEN BREAK YOUR WRISTS EARLY ON THE BACKSWING, HIT FIRMLY, AND TRY TO DELAY THE ROLL OF YOUR WRISTS UNTIL WELL AFTER IMPACT.

Allow for Hook When Ball's Higher

A SIDEHILL SHOT WITH THE BALL HIGH ABOVE YOUR FEET IS ONE OF THE TOUGHEST IN GOLF. BEST POLICY IS TO AVOID SUCH LIES BY SHOOTING FOR LEVEL FAIRWAY AREAS.

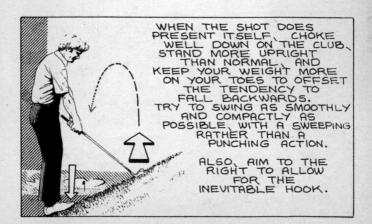

WHEN THE SHOT DOES PRESENT ITSELF, CHOKE WELL DOWN ON THE CLUB, STAND MORE UPRIGHT THAN NORMAL, AND KEEP YOUR WEIGHT MORE ON YOUR TOES TO OFFSET THE TENDENCY TO FALL BACKWARDS. TRY TO SWING AS SMOOTHLY AND COMPACTLY AS POSSIBLE, WITH A SWEEPING RATHER THAN A PUNCHING ACTION.

ALSO, AIM TO THE RIGHT TO ALLOW FOR THE INEVITABLE HOOK.

Allow for Slice When Ball's Lower

A SIDEHILL SHOT WITH THE BALL WELL BELOW YOUR FEET IS ALWAYS A TESTER.

CAREFUL SHOT-PLANNING FROM THE TEE IS THE BEST WAY TO ENSURE YOU DON'T ENCOUNTER TOO MANY OF THESE POTENTIAL SCORE-WRECKERS.

WHEN YOU DO, GRIP THE CLUB AS CLOSE TO THE END AS POSSIBLE, GET WELL DOWN TO THE SHOT BY FLEXING YOUR KNEES, AND PROTECT YOUR BALANCE BY "SITTING ON YOUR HEELS."

SWING COMPACTLY AND RHYTHMICALLY, **STAY DOWN,** AND AIM LEFT TO ALLOW FOR THE LIKELY FADE.

17

Finessing
the Ball

MANY CLUB GOLFERS LACK "BITE" ON THEIR APPROACH SHOTS BECAUSE THEY LACK BACKSPIN.

A SURE REDUCER OF BACKSPIN IS GRASS COMING BETWEEN CLUBFACE AND BALL AT IMPACT, SO CLEAN STRIKING IS YOUR FIRST GOAL.

ANOTHER MIGHT BE TO SWING A LITTLE MORE UPRIGHT, IN THAT THE STEEPER THE ANGLE OF CLUB APPROACH THE MORE POWERFULLY THE BALL WILL BE SPUN UP AND OFF THE CLUBFACE.

HOWEVER, IF YOU GO TO AN UPRIGHT PLANE, BE SURE YOU CONTINUE TO **TURN** AND **EXTEND** FULLY ON THE BACKSWING.

Swing Shorter for "Part" Shots

MANY GOLFERS NEVER TRY ANYTHING LESS THAN A FULL SWING FOR FEAR OF MISSING THE SHOT BY "LETTING UP" ON IT.

BY SO DOING THEY ARE NEEDLESSLY LIMITING THEIR STROKE-MAKING ARSENAL.

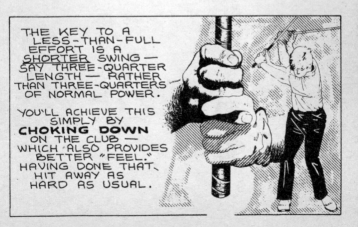

THE KEY TO A LESS-THAN-FULL EFFORT IS A SHORTER SWING — SAY THREE-QUARTER LENGTH — RATHER THAN THREE-QUARTERS OF NORMAL POWER.

YOU'LL ACHIEVE THIS SIMPLY BY **CHOKING DOWN** ON THE CLUB — WHICH ALSO PROVIDES BETTER "FEEL." HAVING DONE THAT, HIT AWAY AS HARD AS USUAL.

"Sweep" Ball with Long Irons

LONG-IRONS AREN'T AS DIFFICULT TO PLAY AS MANY GOLFERS BELIEVE — GIVEN THE RIGHT KIND OF SET-UP AND SWING.

FIRST KEY IS TO POSITION THE BALL FAIRLY WELL FORWARD IN YOUR STANCE, WHERE YOU CAN <u>SWEEP</u> THE CLUBHEAD <u>THROUGH</u> RATHER THAN HITTING DOWN AT THE BALL.

SECOND KEY IS TO SWING ON THE SAME SCALE AND AT THE SAME TEMPO AS YOU SWING A WOODEN CLUB.

THIRD KEY IS TO PRACTICE BOTH TECHNIQUES WITH THE BALL TEED ON A PEG UNTIL YOU BUILD ENOUGH CONFIDENCE IN THE CLUBS TO PLAY THEM FOR REAL OFF THE GROUND.

Waggle as You Want Shot to Fly

YOUR PHYSICAL EXECUTION OF EACH SHOT IS HEAVILY INFLUENCED BY HOW YOU PICTURE IT MENTALLY.

FOR THAT REASON, AND ALSO AS A FORM OF "MINI-REHEARSAL," I WAGGLE AT ADDRESS ACCORDING TO MY INTENDED FLIGHT PATH.

JM

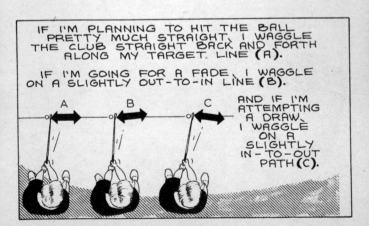

IF I'M PLANNING TO HIT THE BALL PRETTY MUCH STRAIGHT, I WAGGLE THE CLUB STRAIGHT BACK AND FORTH ALONG MY TARGET LINE (A).

IF I'M GOING FOR A FADE, I WAGGLE ON A SLIGHTLY OUT-TO-IN LINE (B).

AND IF I'M ATTEMPTING A DRAW, I WAGGLE ON A SLIGHTLY IN-TO-OUT PATH (C).

A   B   C

THERE ARE TWO WAYS TO INTENTIONALLY SLICE A SHOT. ONE IS TO GRIP WITH THE HANDS FARTHER **LEFT** THAN USUAL, THEN SWING **OUT-TO-IN**.

USE THIS IF IT WORKS FOR YOU, BUT IF NOT, TRY MY WAY.

TO SLICE A SHOT, I SIMPLY <u>OPEN THE CLUBFACE</u> AT ADDRESS, AIM <u>LEFT</u> OF TARGET, THEN SWING <u>NORMALLY</u>.

THE MORE SLICE I WANT, THE MORE I OPEN THE CLUBFACE AND MY SHOULDER ALIGNMENT. THIS WAY I DON'T HAVE TO CHANGE MY BASIC SWING PATTERN.

Understand These "Release" Factors

THE LONGER YOU DELAY THE ROLL OF THE RIGHT FOREARM OVER THE LEFT, THE MORE OPEN THE CLUBFACE WILL BE AND THE BETTER YOUR CHANCES OF FADING OR SLICING THE BALL.

CONVERSELY, THE EARLIER THE WRISTS AND FOREARMS ROTATE THROUGH THE IMPACT ZONE, THE BETTER YOUR CHANCES OF DRAWING OR HOOKING THE BALL BECAUSE OF A CLOSING CLUBFACE. EXPERIMENTING WITH THESE ACTIONS IN PRACTICE IS A FINE WAY TO LEARN SHOT FLIGHTING AND BALL CONTROL.

Use Shaft for High and Low Shots

GOLF OFTEN SEEMS A PARADOXICAL GAME, AND THAT'S NOWHERE MORE TRUE THAN WHEN YOU'RE TRYING TO HIT A HARD LOW SHOT OR A SOFT HIGH SHOT. FOLLOWING THEIR INSTINCTS, MANY GOLFERS HOLD THE CLUB EXACTLY OPPOSITE TO THE CORRECT WAY.

JM

HITTING A HARD LOW SHOT BECOMES MUCH EASIER WHEN YOU **CHOKE DOWN** (A) ON THE CLUB. CONVERSELY, USING **ALL THE SHAFT** (B) MAKES PLAYING A SOFT HIGH SHOT MUCH SIMPLER BY ALLOWING A SLOW TEMPO AND A DELIBERATE SWING.

PROVE THIS TO YOURSELF BY PRACTICING BOTH TECHNIQUES.

A

B

Move Ball _and_ Hand Back for Less Height

MOVING THE BALL BACK IN YOUR STANCE IS CORRECT PROCEDURE ANY TIME YOU WANT TO HIT IT LOWER, BUT ANOTHER ADJUSTMENT IS NECESSARY TO BE SURE YOU GET THE DESIRED FLIGHT.

IF YOU LEAVE YOUR HANDS WHERE THEY NORMALLY ARE AT ADDRESS WHEN MOVING THE BALL BACK, THE EFFECT WILL BE TO CREATE A _STEEPER_ DOWNSWING ARC WHICH WILL CAUSE _MORE_ BACKSPIN AND THUS _GREATER_ RATHER THAN LESSER HEIGHT. SOLUTION IS TO ALSO MOVE YOUR HANDS BACK _PROPORTIONATELY_ TO THE BALL PLACEMENT, THEN SWING NORMALLY.

7-27

Delay Release to Keep Ball Down

YOU'LL KEEP THE BALL **DOWN** MOST EFFECTIVELY WITH A SLIGHTLY CLOSED CLUBFACE DELIVERY AND A DELAYED RELEASE OF THE CLUBHEAD.

FOR A LOW SHOT, POSITION THE BALL A LITTLE FARTHER BACK IN YOUR STANCE AND HOOD THE CLUBFACE SLIGHTLY.

THEN DELAY THE CLUBHEAD RELEASE BY LEADING THE THROUGH-SWING WITH YOUR LEGS WHILE KEEPING YOUR WRISTS FIRM.

STAY DOWN ON THE SHOT, AND ALLOW FOR A DRAW.

Release Freely to Hit Ball High

HEIGHT IS MOST EASILY ACHIEVED BY A SLIGHTLY <u>OPEN</u> CLUBFACE DELIVERY, COMBINED WITH A <u>VIGOROUS</u> <u>RELEASE</u> OF THE CLUBHEAD THROUGH THE BALL.

WHEN YOU NEED A PARTICULARLY HIGH SHOT, SET THE BALL A LITTLE FARTHER FORWARD IN YOUR STANCE AND OPEN THE CLUBFACE A FEW DEGREES.

THEN BE SURE TO <u>RELEASE</u> THE CLUBHEAD — UNCOCK YOUR WRISTS — FULLY THROUGH IMPACT. STAY <u>BEHIND</u> THE BALL AND ALLOW FOR A LITTLE FADE.

JM

18

Practice

If You Want to Improve—Practice!

WHAT MAKES A GOOD GOLFER?

ATHLETICISM, COORDINATION, DESIRE, INTELLIGENCE, SELF-CONTROL ARE ALL FACTORS — PERHAPS INDISPENSABLE ONES FOR ANYONE WHO SEEKS TO ACHIEVE THE HIGHEST LEVELS OF THE GAME TODAY.

BUT THERE'S ANOTHER FACTOR, TOO — PRACTICE. THERE'S NEVER BEEN A TOP PLAYER WHO DID NOT HIT TENS OF THOUSANDS OF PRACTICE SHOTS BOTH IN LEARNING AND SUSTAINING HIS OR HER GAME. THE REASON IS THAT THIS IS THE ONLY WAY TO ENSURE THAT FINE SHOTS CAN BE PRODUCED "AUTOMATICALLY" — WHICH IS THE BIG DIFFERENCE BETWEEN THE GOOD CLUB GOLFER AND THOSE WHO PLAY GOLF FOR A LIVING.

Work Most on One Basic "Shape"

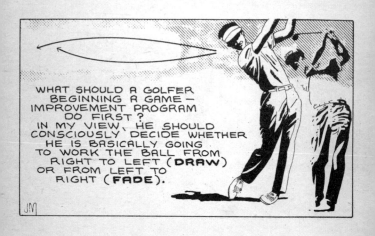

WHAT SHOULD A GOLFER
BEGINNING A GAME-
IMPROVEMENT PROGRAM
DO FIRST?
IN MY VIEW, HE SHOULD
CONSCIOUSLY DECIDE WHETHER
HE IS BASICALLY GOING
TO WORK THE BALL FROM
RIGHT TO LEFT (**DRAW**)
OR FROM LEFT TO
RIGHT (**FADE**).

A DEAD STRAIGHT SHOT IS THE TOUGHEST
TO HIT ONCE, LET ALONE TO REPEAT
CONTINUALLY. FOR THAT AND ALSO FOR
STRATEGICAL REASONS, ALMOST ALL
TOUR PROS DELIBERATELY EITHER
DRAW OR FADE MOST OF THEIR LONG
SHOTS. THAT'S HOW YOU
SHOULD LEARN TO PLAY GOLF,
TOO.

(EVENTUALLY, OF COURSE, IF
YOU'RE REALLY SERIOUS
ABOUT THE GAME, YOU SHOULD
LEARN TO HIT
BOTH WAYS
AT WILL.)

Keep Those Legs Strong

GOOD GOLF IS IMPOSSIBLE IF YOUR LEGS ARE IN LOUSY SHAPE, SO BEING AS ACTIVE AS YOU CAN OFF THE COURSE IS DEFINITELY GOING TO INCREASE YOUR PROWESS AND YOUR PLEASURE ON IT.

GOLF HAS NEVER PROVIDED ME WITH VIGOROUS ENOUGH EXERCISE TO STAY IN THE SHAPE I FEEL NECESSARY TO BE FULLY COMPETITIVE, SO I LIKE TO PLAY MORE STRENUOUS SPORTS AS OFTEN AS POSSIBLE. THE COMPETITION INVOLVED HELPS KEEP ME SHARP FOR GOLF, TOO.

Build Your Game off The Course

ANY TIME YOU CAN'T GET TO THE COURSE FOR A LENGTHY SPELL, DO YOUR DARNDEST TO KEEP AS MANY OF YOUR GOLFING MUSCLES AS POSSIBLE IN THE BEST SHAPE YOU CAN.

IT MIGHT MAKE YOU SWEAT A LITTLE, BUT IT'LL PAY OFF COME PAY-UP TIME!

JOHN SMITH

JM

DO A FEW STRETCHING, BENDING AND TWISTING EXERCISES EACH MORNING FOR THE LOWER BACK AND TORSO. WALK INSTEAD OF RIDING AND TAKE THE STAIRS OVER THE ELEVATOR WHENEVER YOU CAN.

ABOVE ALL, TRY TO SWING A CLUB SOMEWHERE PERIODICALLY — AND PREFERABLY A WEIGHTED ONE.

Practice One Thing at a Time

YOU'LL PRACTICE MORE EFFECTIVELY IF YOU CONCENTRATE ON ONE AREA OF THE SWING AT A TIME.

THE FIRST PRIORITIES ARE WHAT MIGHT BE CALLED THE 'STATIC' FUNDAMENTALS — GRIP, AIM AND STANCE, HEAD POSITION, BALL POSITION, AND ADDRESS POSTURE.

ONLY MOVE ON TO THE "ACTION" FUNDAMENTALS WHEN YOU FEEL YOU HAVE THESE 'STATICS' RIGHT. THE ACTION FUNDAMENTALS, TO ME, ARE FULL BACKSWING TURN, HIGH HANDS AT THE TOP, BEGINNING THE DOWNSWING WITH THE LOWER BODY, RELEASING THE CLUBHEAD FULLY, AND SMOOTH OVERALL TEMPO.

Practice on the Course, Too

FIND PRACTICING ON A DRIVING RANGE BORING?

OKAY, THEN DO YOUR PRACTICING ON THE COURSE.

PLAY ALONE WHENEVER THE COURSE ISN'T TOO BUSY, HITTING TWO OR THREE BALLS ON EACH HOLE.

PLAYING EACH BALL AGAINST THE OTHER IS ONE WAY TO MAINTAIN YOUR INTEREST. ANOTHER IS TO TAKE OUT ONLY A FEW CLUBS AND LEARN HOW TO "MANUFACTURE" SHOTS — A GREAT WAY TO DEVELOP FINESSE. ALSO, WALK RATHER THAN RIDE ON THESE OUTINGS, BECAUSE THE EXTRA MILEAGE YOU COVER HITTING A NUMBER OF BALLS WILL DO WONDERS FOR YOUR LEGS.

Warm Up Before You Play

YOU'LL RARELY SEE A HANDICAP GOLFER HIT WARM-UP SHOTS BEFORE HE RUSHES TO THE FIRST TEE. YOU'LL RARELY SEE A PROFESSIONAL <u>NOT</u> DO SO.

MAYBE THAT HAS A LITTLE SOMETHING TO DO WITH THE WAY EACH PLAYS.

START A WARM-UP SESSION WITH A SHORT-IRON AND THEN HIT A FEW SHOTS WITH EVERY SECOND OR THIRD CLUB.

DON'T OVERDO IT!

REMEMBER, YOU'RE WARMING UP, NOT REBUILDING YOUR SWING!

Don't Be Overambitious
After Lay-off

TOUGHEST THING TO RECAPTURE AFTER A LONG LAYOFF FROM GOLF IS GOOD SWING TEMPO. GENERALLY, BEING OUT OF PRACTICE AND MAYBE LACKING CONFIDENCE, YOU'LL TEND TO BE JERKY AND FAST.

TO REFIND YOUR TEMPO — AND WITH IT "FEEL" AND CONFIDENCE — DON'T BE TOO AMBITIOUS ON THE PRACTICE RANGE: CONCENTRATE ON BASIC SWING FUNDAMENTALS RATHER THAN WHERE OR HOW FAR THE BALL GOES. AND KEEP EVERYTHING SIMPLE FOR A WHILE, TOO, SAVING THE FANCY SHOTS AND THE FINESSE STROKES UNTIL YOU'VE GOT THE BASICS DOWN PAT AGAIN.

Practice "Finessing" the Ball

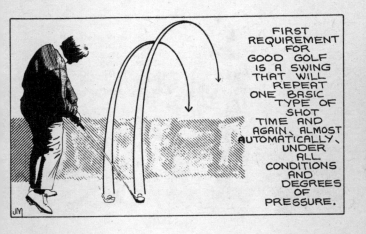

FIRST REQUIREMENT FOR GOOD GOLF IS A SWING THAT WILL REPEAT ONE BASIC TYPE OF SHOT TIME AND AGAIN, ALMOST AUTOMATICALLY, UNDER ALL CONDITIONS AND DEGREES OF PRESSURE.

NEXT REQUIREMENT IS THE ABILITY TO "FINESSE" THE BALL — TO FIT SPECIAL SHOTS TO SPECIAL CIRCUMSTANCES. ADDING THIS CAPABILITY TO ONE'S ARMORY TAKES IMAGINATION AND A CERTAIN AMOUNT OF TRIAL AND ERROR. BUT MOST OF ALL IT TAKES PRACTICE — LOTS AND LOTS OF PRACTICE. SO ALWAYS TRY TO INCLUDE SOME NON-STANDARD OR "TYPE" SHOTS IN YOUR GAME-BUILDING SESSIONS.

Work on Balance This Way

BEST WAY I KNOW TO DEVELOP BALANCE — AND ALSO A GOOD HEAD STEADIER — IS TO PRACTICE SWINGING FROM THE <u>INSIDES</u> OF THE FEET.

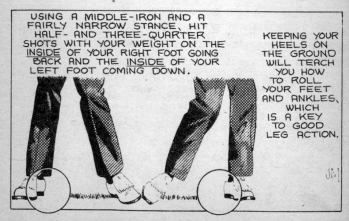

USING A MIDDLE-IRON AND A FAIRLY NARROW STANCE, HIT HALF- AND THREE-QUARTER SHOTS WITH YOUR WEIGHT ON THE <u>INSIDE</u> OF YOUR RIGHT FOOT GOING BACK AND THE <u>INSIDE</u> OF YOUR LEFT FOOT COMING DOWN.

KEEPING YOUR HEELS ON THE GROUND WILL TEACH YOU HOW TO ROLL YOUR FEET AND ANKLES, WHICH IS A KEY TO GOOD LEG ACTION.

Learn to Play Less Than Full Shots

THERE'S NO DOUBT AMPLE SHORT-IRON PRACTICE WILL IMPROVE YOUR SCORING FASTER THAN MOST OTHER TRAINING REGIMENS. BUT THE IMPROVE- MENT WILL BE EVEN GREATER YET IF YOU INCLUDE PLENTY OF 'FINESSE' SHOTS IN THESE SESSIONS.

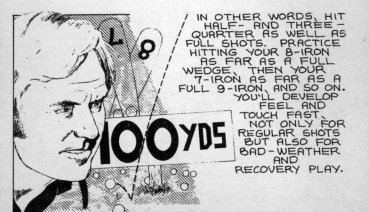

IN OTHER WORDS, HIT HALF- AND THREE- QUARTER AS WELL AS FULL SHOTS. PRACTICE HITTING YOUR 8-IRON AS FAR AS A FULL WEDGE, THEN YOUR 7-IRON AS FAR AS A FULL 9-IRON, AND SO ON. YOU'LL DEVELOP FEEL AND TOUCH FAST, NOT ONLY FOR REGULAR SHOTS BUT ALSO FOR BAD-WEATHER AND RECOVERY PLAY.

100YDS

Work on _All_ Facets of the Game

WANT TO IMPROVE FAST AT GOLF??
IF YOU CAN'T BREAK 100 BUT ARE CLOSE, A COUPLE OF LESSONS WOULD ALMOST CERTAINLY MOVE YOU INTO THE 90s.

IF YOU'RE A 90s-SHOOTER YEARNING FOR THE 80s, WORKING ON YOUR SHORT GAME WILL GET YOU THERE FASTEST.

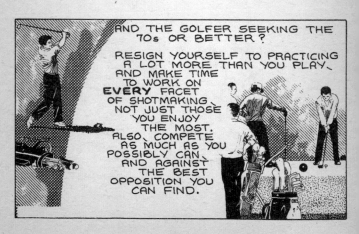

AND THE GOLFER SEEKING THE 70s OR BETTER?

RESIGN YOURSELF TO PRACTICING A LOT MORE THAN YOU PLAY, AND MAKE TIME TO WORK ON **EVERY** FACET OF SHOTMAKING, NOT JUST THOSE YOU ENJOY THE MOST. ALSO, COMPETE AS MUCH AS YOU POSSIBLY CAN, AND AGAINST THE BEST OPPOSITION YOU CAN FIND.